THE STEM FILES

TOP SECRET: PHARMER

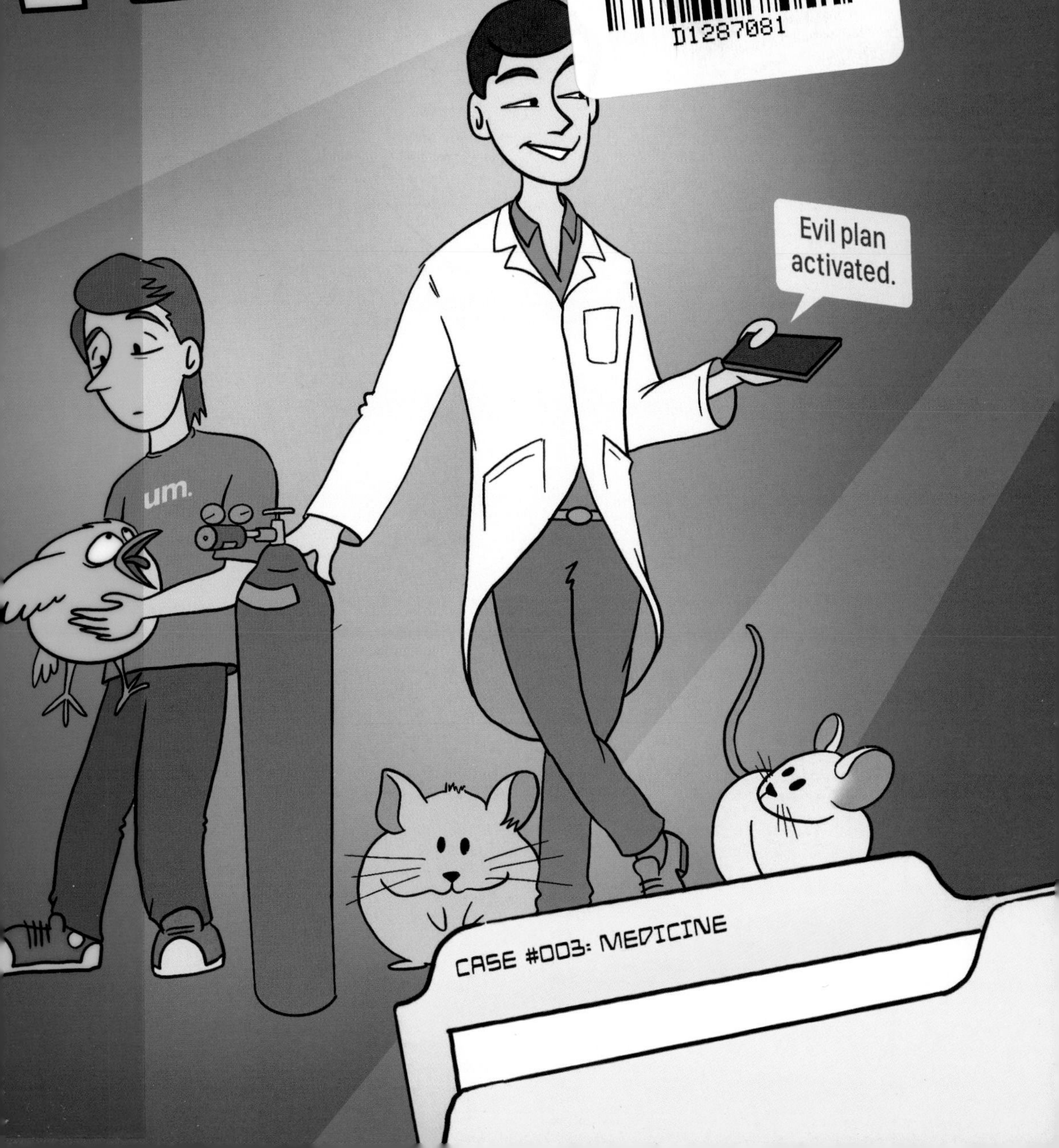
Evil plan activated.
um.
CASE #003: MEDICINE

TORCH GRAPHIC PRESS

Published in the United States of America by Cherry Lake Publishing Group
Ann Arbor, Michigan
www.cherrylakepublishing.com

Story & Illustrator: D.C. London
Character Design: John Boissy
Reading Adviser: Marla Conn, MS, Ed., Literacy specialist, Read-Ability, Inc.
Content Adviser: Stacy Chin, PhD
Production Artists: Jen Wahi, Mary Wagner, Jessica Rogner

Torch Graphic Press is an imprint of Cherry Lake Publishing Group.

Library of Congress Cataloging-in-Publication Data

Names: London, D. C., author.
Title: Top secret: Pharmer / by D.C. London.
Other titles: Pharmer
Description: Ann Arbor, Michigan : Cherry Lake Publishing, [2020] | Series:
   The STEM files | Includes bibliographical references and index. |
Identifiers: LCCN 2020006937 (print) | LCCN 2020006938 (ebook) | ISBN
   9781534169371 (hardcover) | ISBN 9781534171053 (paperback) | ISBN
   9781534172890 (pdf) | ISBN 9781534174733 (ebook)
Subjects: LCSH: Graphic novels. | CYAC: Graphic novels. |
   Bacteria--Fiction. | Cold (Disease)--Fiction. | Villains--Fiction.
Classification: LCC PZ7.7.L663 Tok 2020 (print) | LCC PZ7.7.L663 (ebook)
   | DDC 741.5/973--dc23
LC record available at https://lccn.loc.gov/2020006937
LC ebook record available at https://lccn.loc.gov/2020006938

Cherry Lake Publishing Group would like to acknowledge the work of the
Partnership for 21st Century Learning, a Network of Battelle for Kids.
Please visit http://www.battelleforkids.org/networks/p21 for more information.

Printed in the United States of America
Corporate Graphics

About the Artist: D.C. London

Mr. London is an author, illustrator, designer, part-time Samurai, Army veteran, former rocket scientist, and tank blower-upper. He blatantly violates child labor laws by forcing his three young sons to read his silly books and tests bad jokes on them without proper protective gear.

Table of Contents

A Note on STEM and Medicine
STEM stands for science, technology, engineering, and mathematics. In this book, you will learn about the different types of medicine, how they affect the body, and the importance of ethics in medical research.

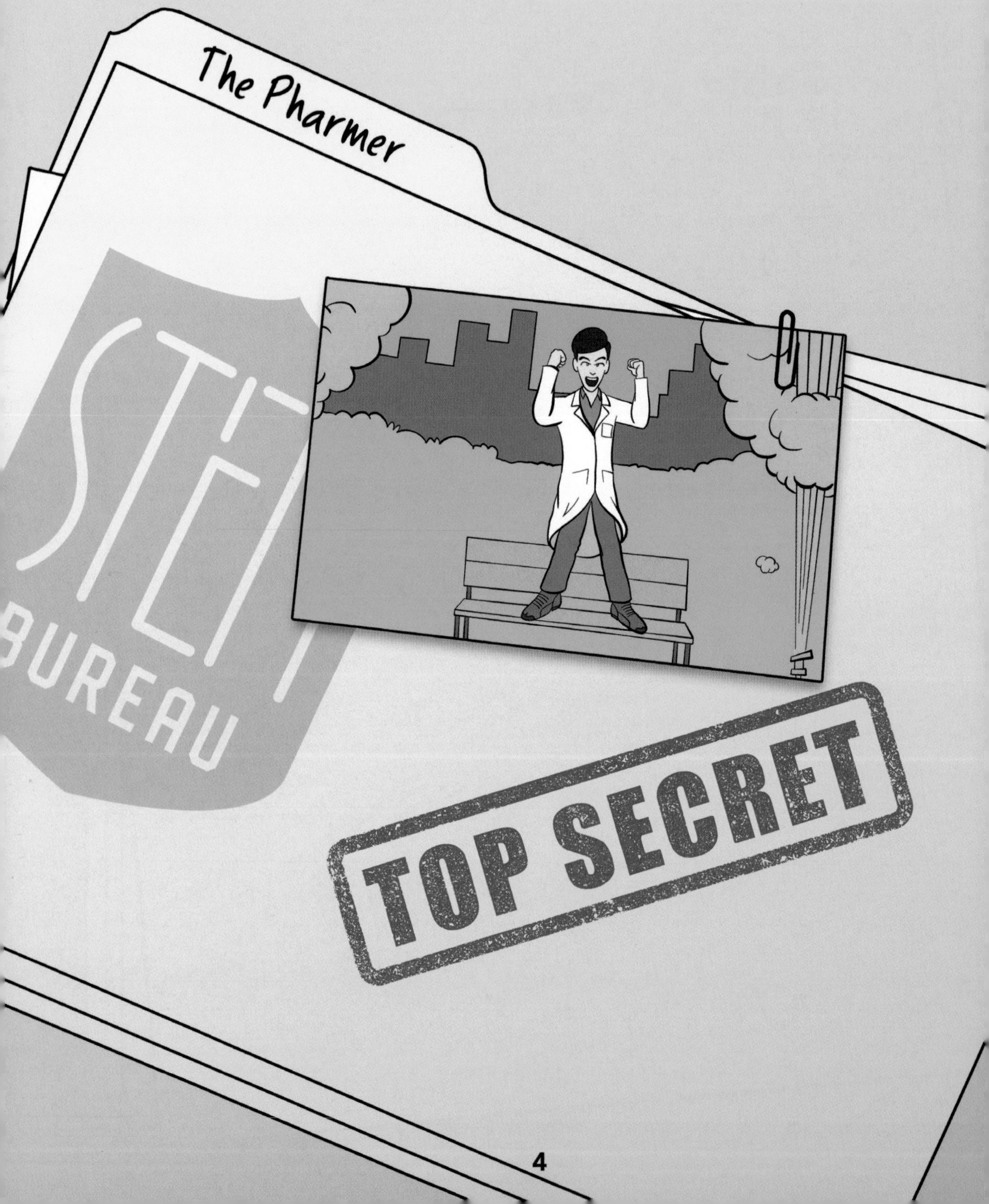
The Pharmer
BUREAU
TOP SECRET

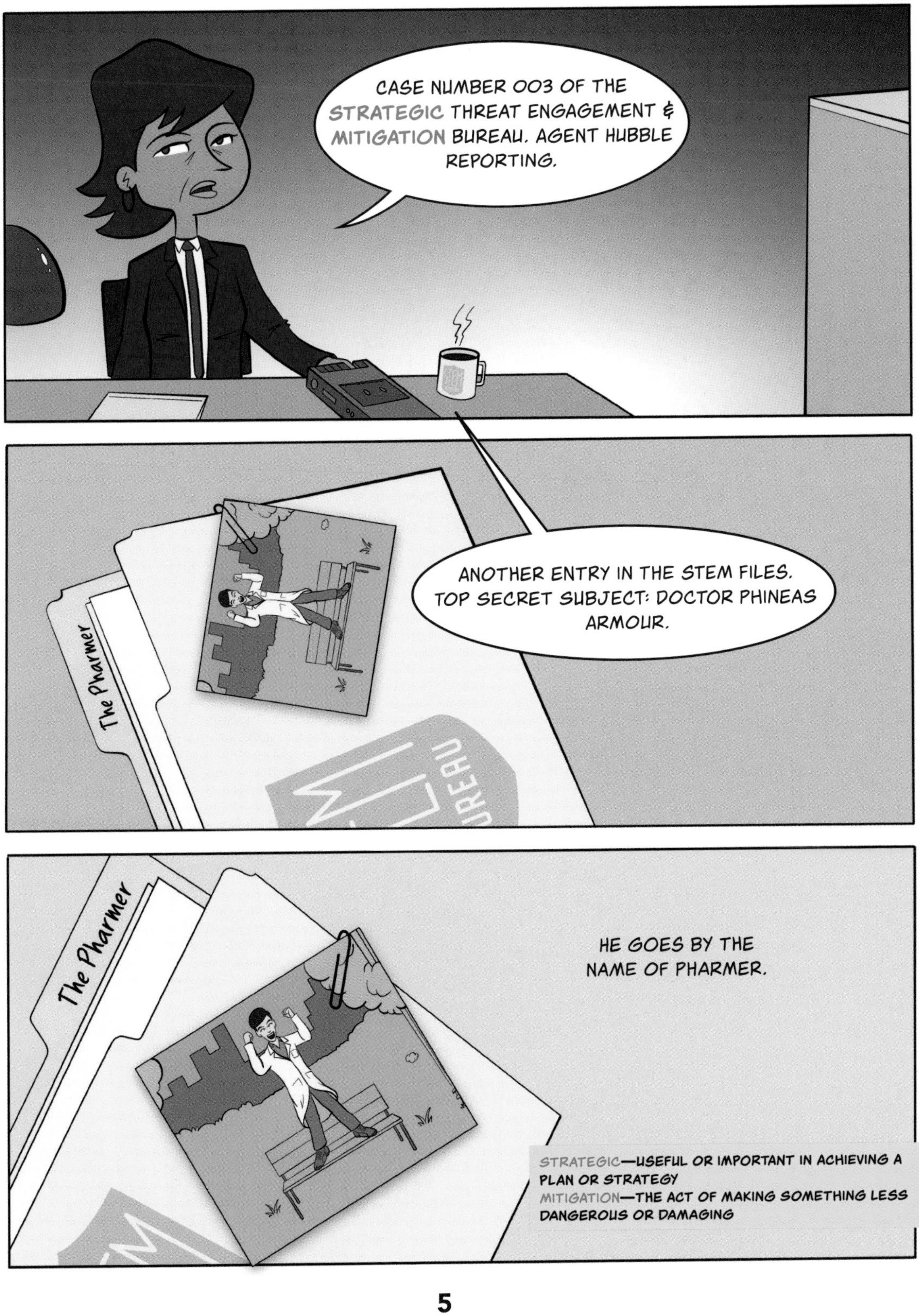
CASE NUMBER 003 OF THE STRATEGIC THREAT ENGAGEMENT & MITIGATION BUREAU. AGENT HUBBLE REPORTING.
STEM
ANOTHER ENTRY IN THE STEM FILES. TOP SECRET SUBJECT: DOCTOR PHINEAS ARMOUR.
The Pharmer
BUREAU
The Pharmer
HE GOES BY THE NAME OF PHARMER.

STRATEGIC—USEFUL OR IMPORTANT IN ACHIEVING A PLAN OR STRATEGY
MITIGATION—THE ACT OF MAKING SOMETHING LESS DANGEROUS OR DAMAGING

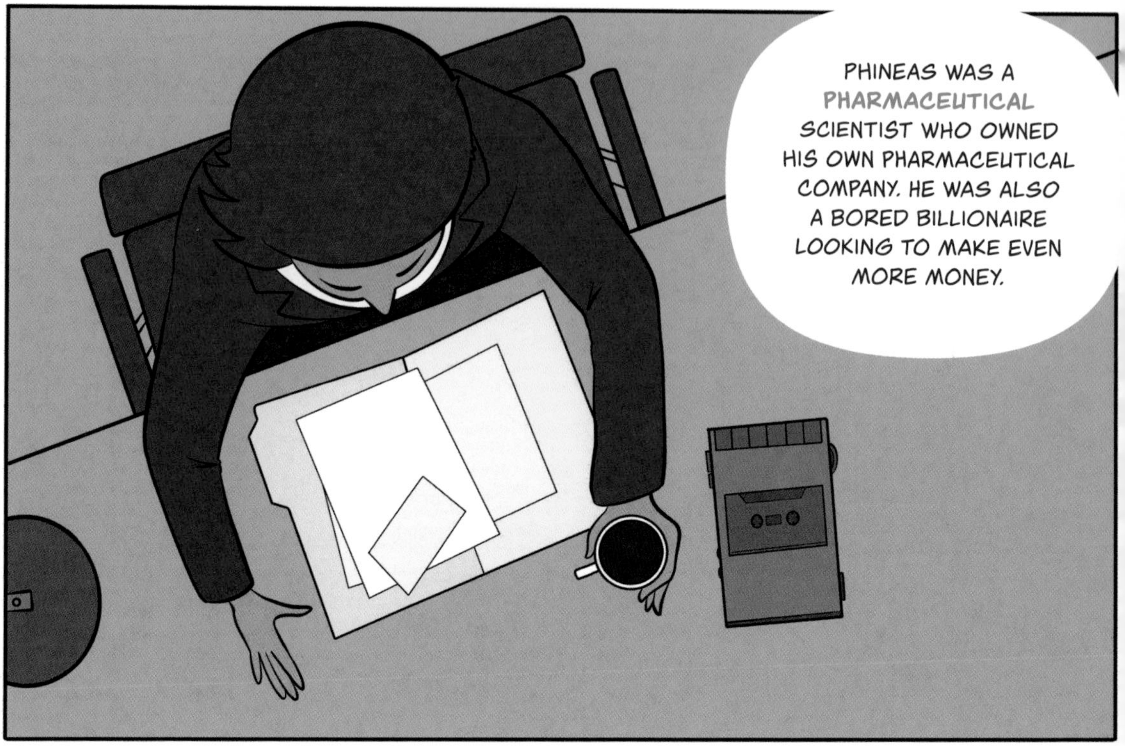
PHINEAS WAS A PHARMACEUTICAL SCIENTIST WHO OWNED HIS OWN PHARMACEUTICAL COMPANY. HE WAS ALSO A BORED BILLIONAIRE LOOKING TO MAKE EVEN MORE MONEY.

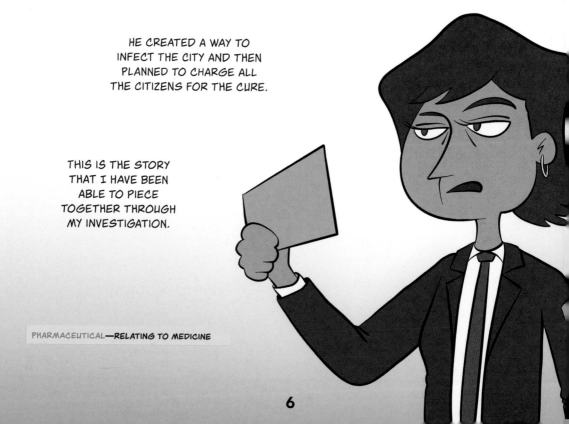

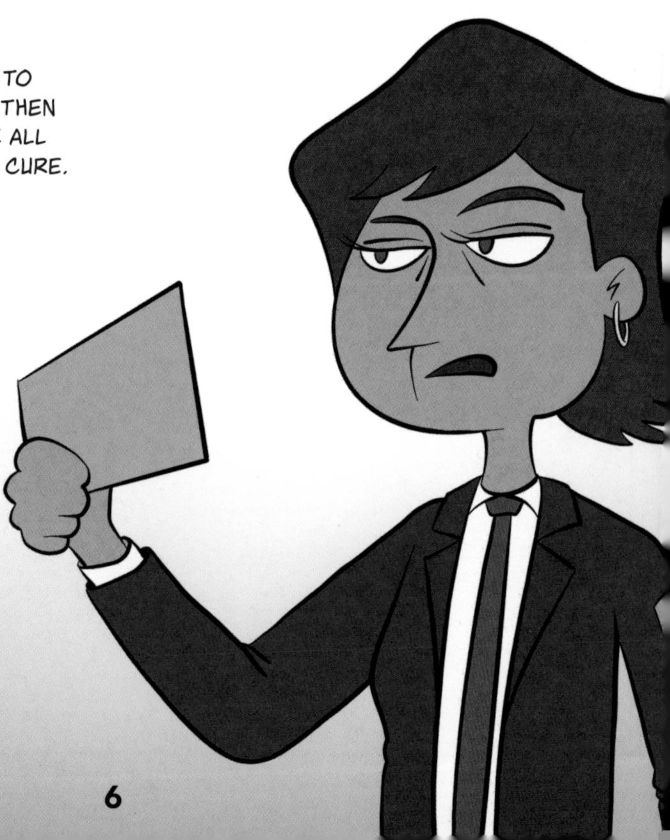
HE CREATED A WAY TO INFECT THE CITY AND THEN PLANNED TO CHARGE ALL THE CITIZENS FOR THE CURE.
THIS IS THE STORY THAT I HAVE BEEN ABLE TO PIECE TOGETHER THROUGH MY INVESTIGATION.

PHARMACEUTICAL—**RELATING TO MEDICINE**

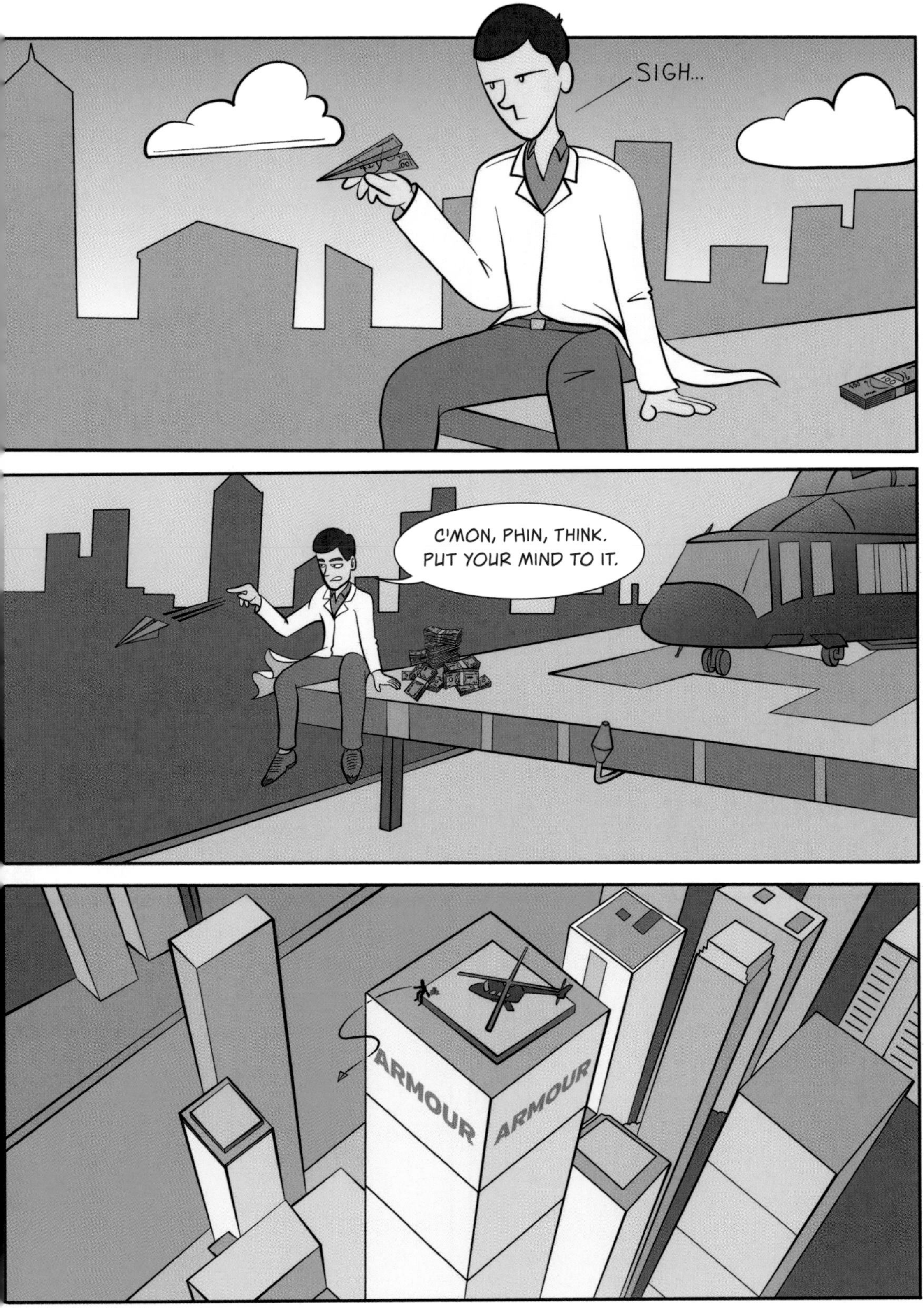
SIGH...
C'MON, PHIN, THINK. PUT YOUR MIND TO IT.
ARMOUR
ARMOUR

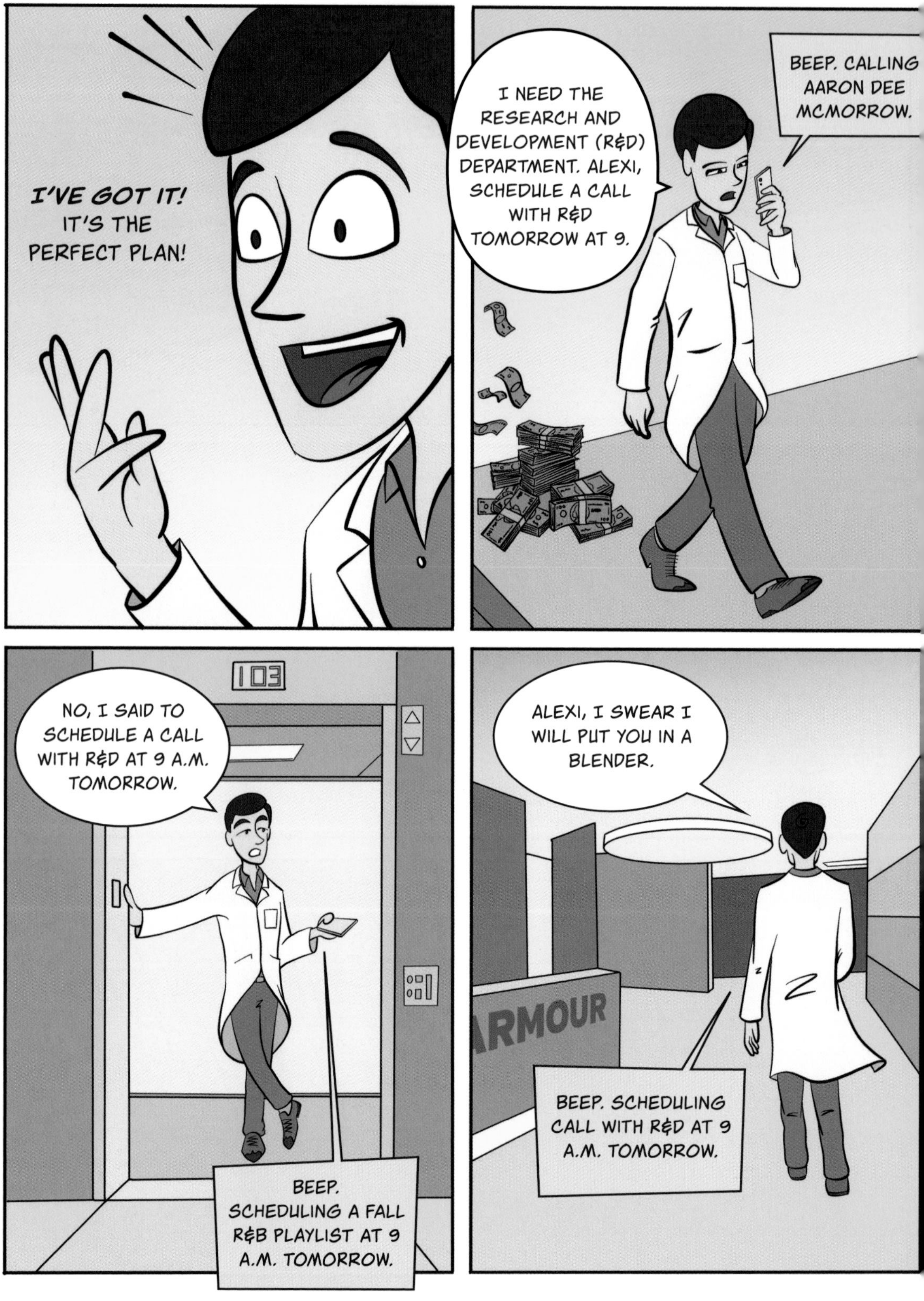
I'VE GOT IT! IT'S THE PERFECT PLAN!
I NEED THE RESEARCH AND DEVELOPMENT (R&D) DEPARTMENT. ALEXI, SCHEDULE A CALL WITH R&D TOMORROW AT 9.
BEEP. CALLING AARON DEE MCMORROW.
103
NO, I SAID TO SCHEDULE A CALL WITH R&D AT 9 A.M. TOMORROW.
BEEP. SCHEDULING A FALL R&B PLAYLIST AT 9 A.M. TOMORROW.
ALEXI, I SWEAR I WILL PUT YOU IN A BLENDER.
ARMOUR
BEEP. SCHEDULING CALL WITH R&D AT 9 A.M. TOMORROW.

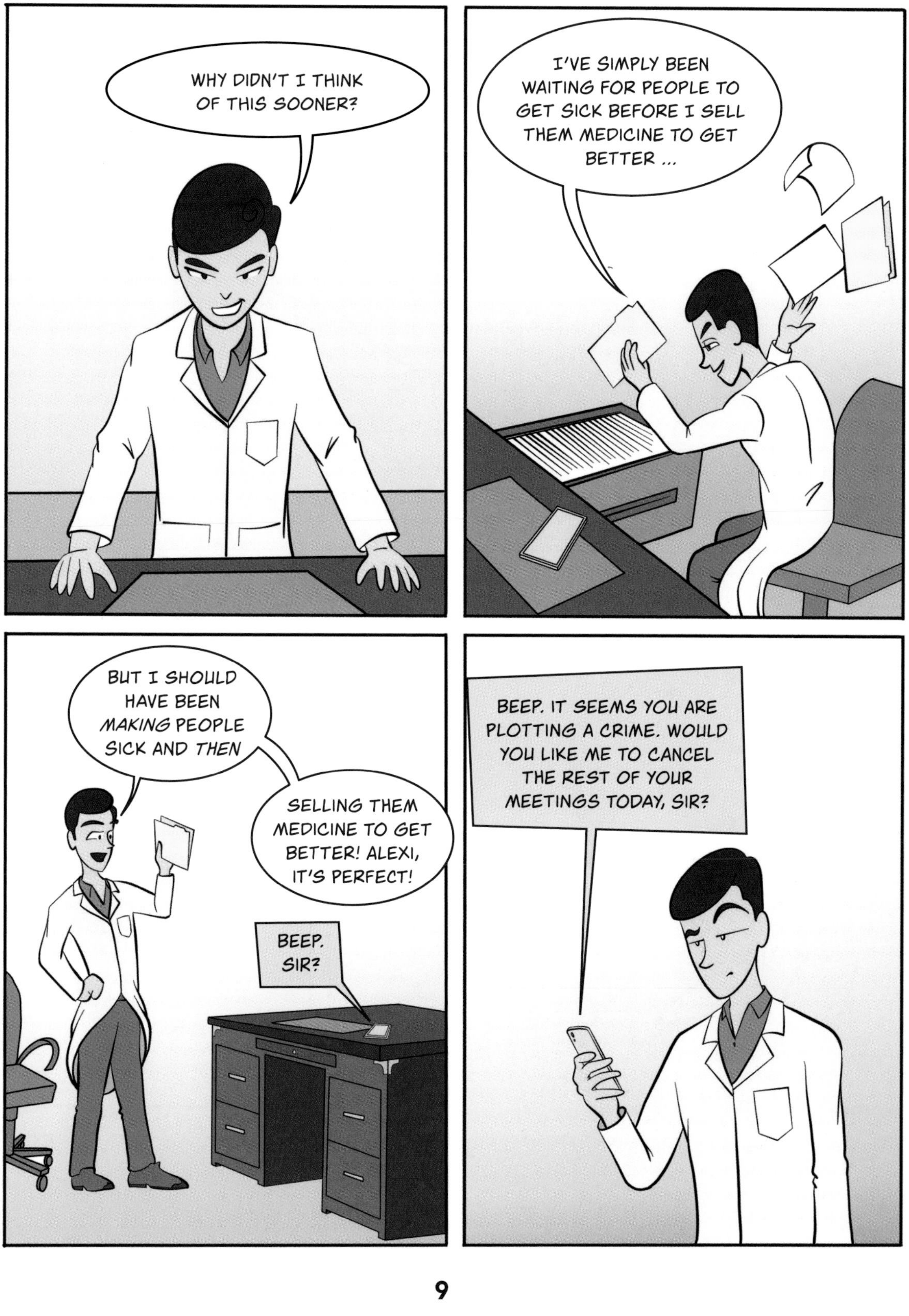
WHY DIDN'T I THINK OF THIS SOONER?
I'VE SIMPLY BEEN WAITING FOR PEOPLE TO GET SICK BEFORE I SELL THEM MEDICINE TO GET BETTER ...
BUT I SHOULD HAVE BEEN *MAKING* PEOPLE SICK AND *THEN*
SELLING THEM MEDICINE TO GET BETTER! ALEXI, IT'S PERFECT!
BEEP. SIR?
BEEP. IT SEEMS YOU ARE PLOTTING A CRIME. WOULD YOU LIKE ME TO CANCEL THE REST OF YOUR MEETINGS TODAY, SIR?

TESTING LAB
HOW DO YOU NOT UNDERSTAND? I SAID I WANT YOU TO REVERSE ENGINEER OUR COLD MEDICINE TO MAKE PEOPLE COLDER! ER, I MEAN SICKER.
OKAY, BOSS. NOT SURE WHY, BUT YEAH, WE'LL GET RIGHT ON THAT.
AND I WANT IT AEROSOLIZED, LIKE ASTHMA INHALERS. MAKE IT A GAS SO PEOPLE BREATHE IT IN.
OH! AND MAKE IT SMELL LIKE STRAWBERRIES.
YOU HAVE A WEEK.

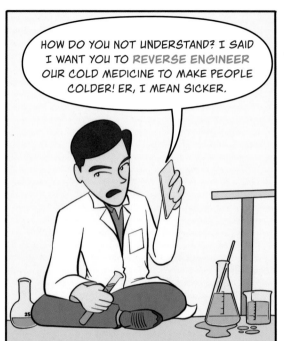

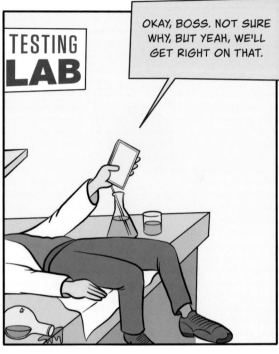

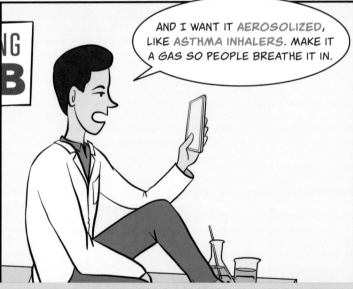

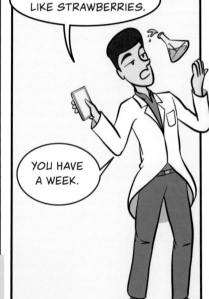

REVERSE ENGINEER—TO STUDY THE PARTS OF SOMETHING IN ORDER TO KNOW HOW IT IS MADE AND HOW IT WORKS
AEROSOLIZED—MADE INTO PARTICLES SMALL ENOUGH TO MOVE THROUGH THE AIR
ASTHMA INHALERS—PORTABLE MEDICAL DEVICES USED FOR DELIVERING MEDICINE THAT TREATS A LUNG DISEASE CALLED ASTHMA

The common cold is caused by many different viruses. Since there is no single virus responsible, it is very challenging to develop a cure. This is why cold medicine can only help to relieve symptoms but cannot cure the common cold itself!

Types of Medicine

The main types of medicine are capsules, inhalers, creams, and vaccinations. Medicines come in many different formats and have to target different areas of the body—the digestive system, the cardiovascular system, or the nervous system. To make sure the medications are delivered most effectively, they have to be prepared in different forms. The medical issue a patient is dealing with determines what type of medicine a doctor will give.

For example, some medicines are in the form of a capsule since they must be swallowed and digested to work inside your body. These capsules contain medicine in a small plastic shell that dissolves slowly in the stomach. Other times, medicine needs to be released directly into the lungs, which can be done with an inhaler. Medicine can also be mixed into a cream to help it be absorbed into the skin. Vaccinations are medicines that have to be injected into the muscle or bloodstream.

um.

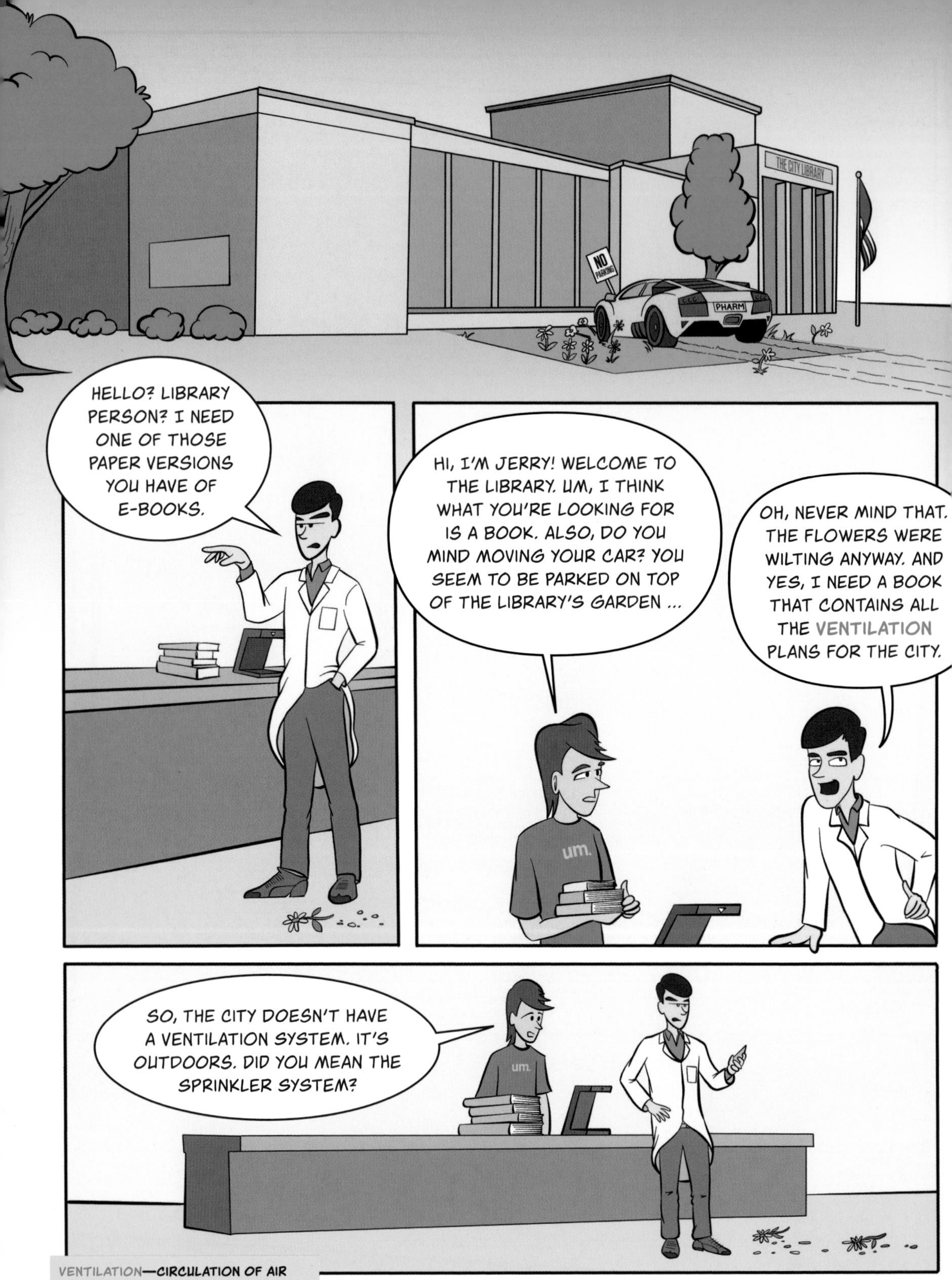
THE CITY LIBRARY
NO PARKING
PHARM
HELLO? LIBRARY PERSON? I NEED ONE OF THOSE PAPER VERSIONS YOU HAVE OF E-BOOKS.
HI, I'M JERRY! WELCOME TO THE LIBRARY. UM, I THINK WHAT YOU'RE LOOKING FOR IS A BOOK. ALSO, DO YOU MIND MOVING YOUR CAR? YOU SEEM TO BE PARKED ON TOP OF THE LIBRARY'S GARDEN ...
um.
OH, NEVER MIND THAT. THE FLOWERS WERE WILTING ANYWAY. AND YES, I NEED A BOOK THAT CONTAINS ALL THE VENTILATION PLANS FOR THE CITY.
SO, THE CITY DOESN'T HAVE A VENTILATION SYSTEM. IT'S OUTDOORS. DID YOU MEAN THE SPRINKLER SYSTEM?
um.

VENTILATION—CIRCULATION OF AIR

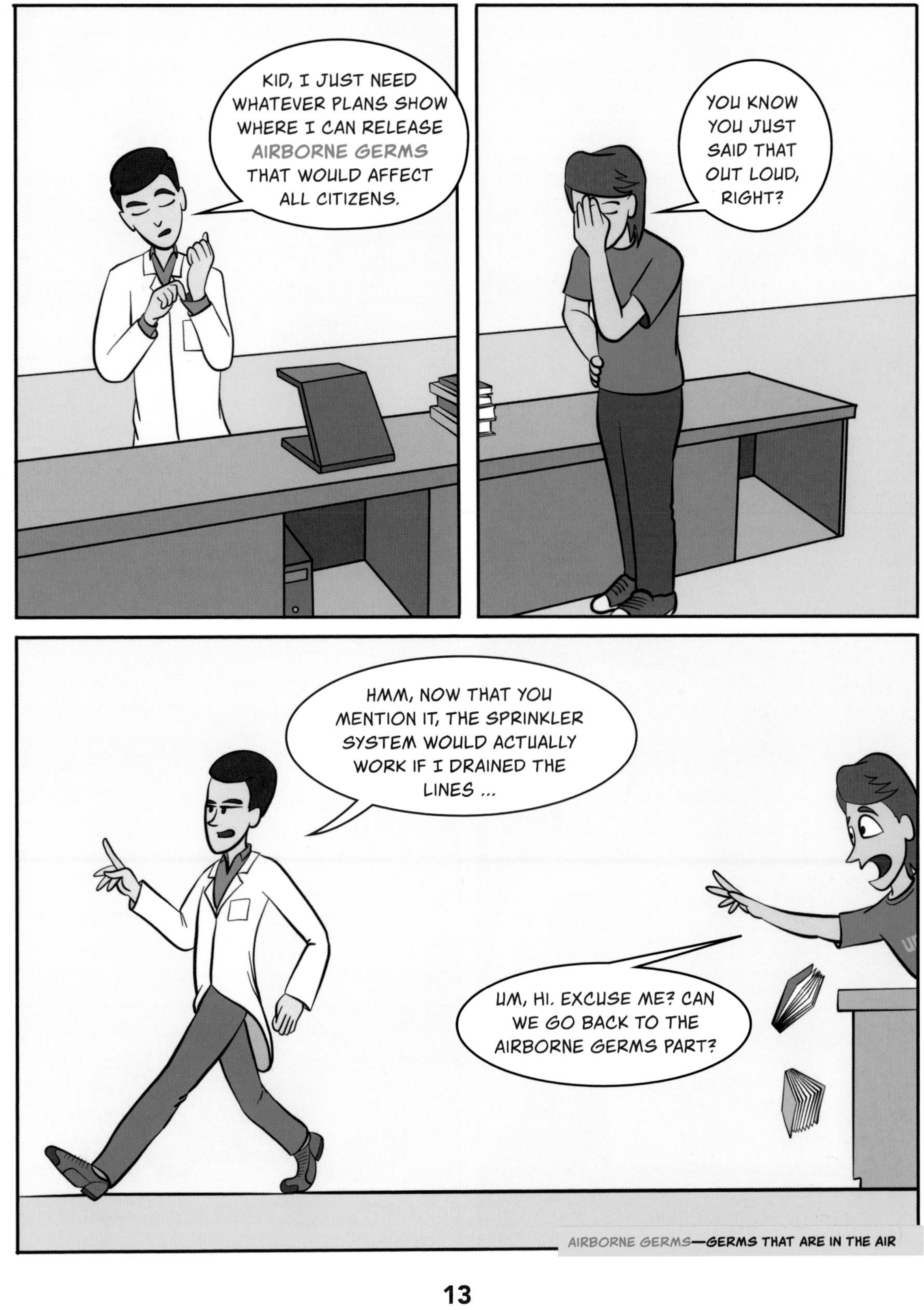
KID, I JUST NEED WHATEVER PLANS SHOW WHERE I CAN RELEASE AIRBORNE GERMS THAT WOULD AFFECT ALL CITIZENS.
YOU KNOW YOU JUST SAID THAT OUT LOUD, RIGHT?
HMM, NOW THAT YOU MENTION IT, THE SPRINKLER SYSTEM WOULD ACTUALLY WORK IF I DRAINED THE LINES ...
UM, HI. EXCUSE ME? CAN WE GO BACK TO THE AIRBORNE GERMS PART?

AIRBORNE GERMS—GERMS THAT ARE IN THE AIR

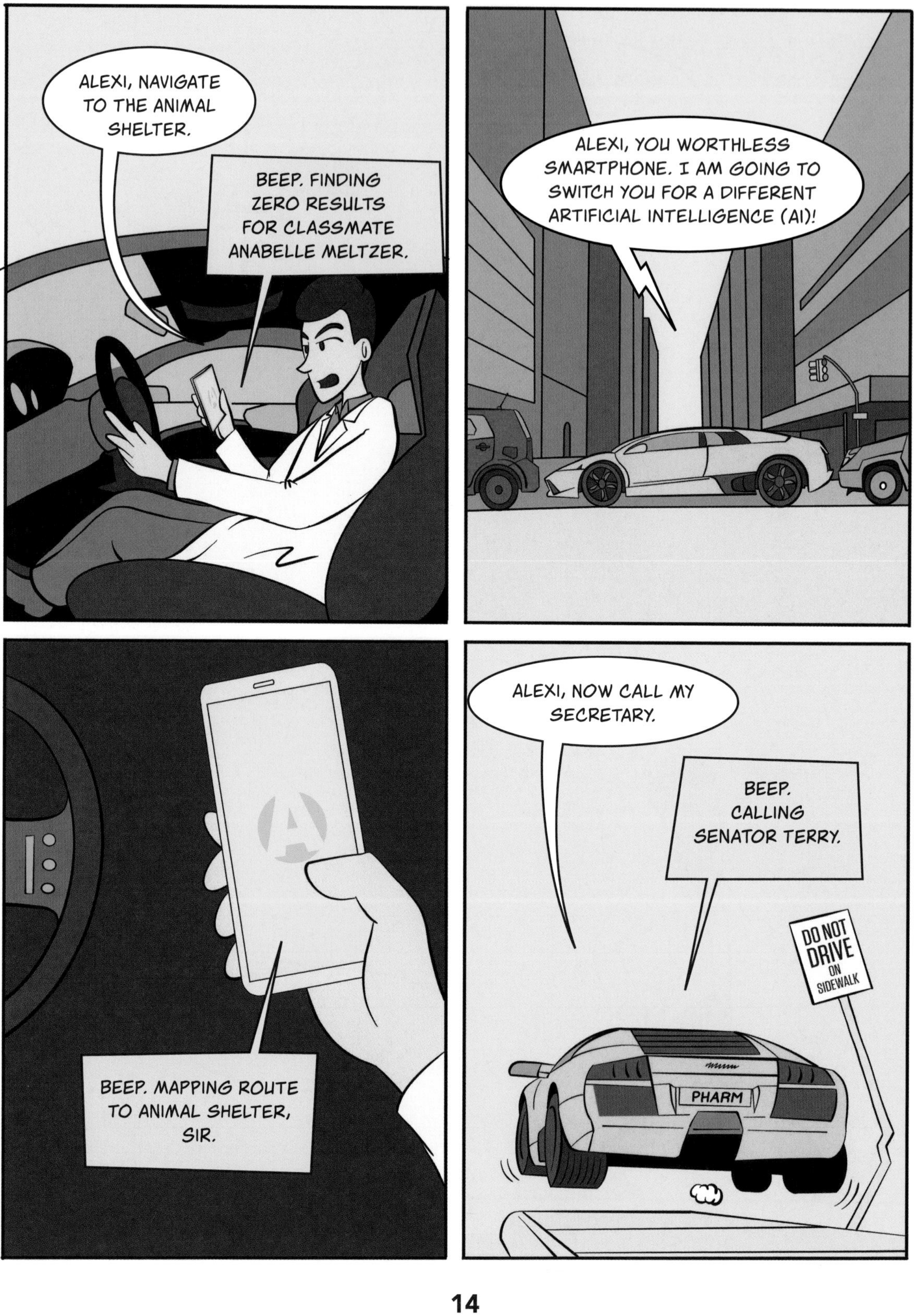
ALEXI, NAVIGATE TO THE ANIMAL SHELTER.
BEEP. FINDING ZERO RESULTS FOR CLASSMATE ANABELLE MELTZER.
ALEXI, YOU WORTHLESS SMARTPHONE. I AM GOING TO SWITCH YOU FOR A DIFFERENT ARTIFICIAL INTELLIGENCE (AI)!
BEEP. MAPPING ROUTE TO ANIMAL SHELTER, SIR.
ALEXI, NOW CALL MY SECRETARY.
BEEP. CALLING SENATOR TERRY.
DO NOT DRIVE ON SIDEWALK
PHARM

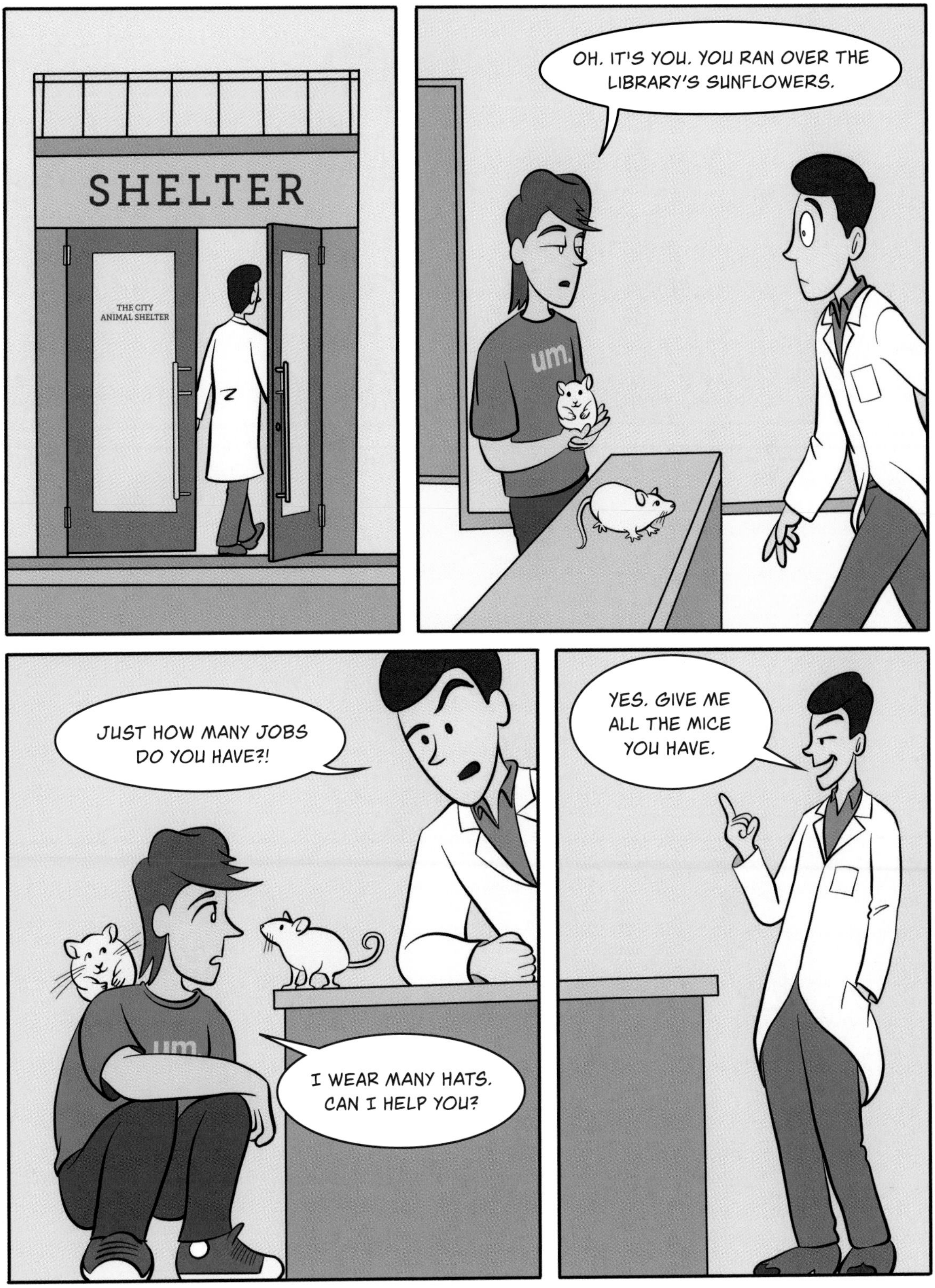
SHELTER
THE CITY ANIMAL SHELTER
OH. IT'S YOU. YOU RAN OVER THE LIBRARY'S SUNFLOWERS.
um.
JUST HOW MANY JOBS DO YOU HAVE?!
I WEAR MANY HATS. CAN I HELP YOU?
um.
YES. GIVE ME ALL THE MICE YOU HAVE.

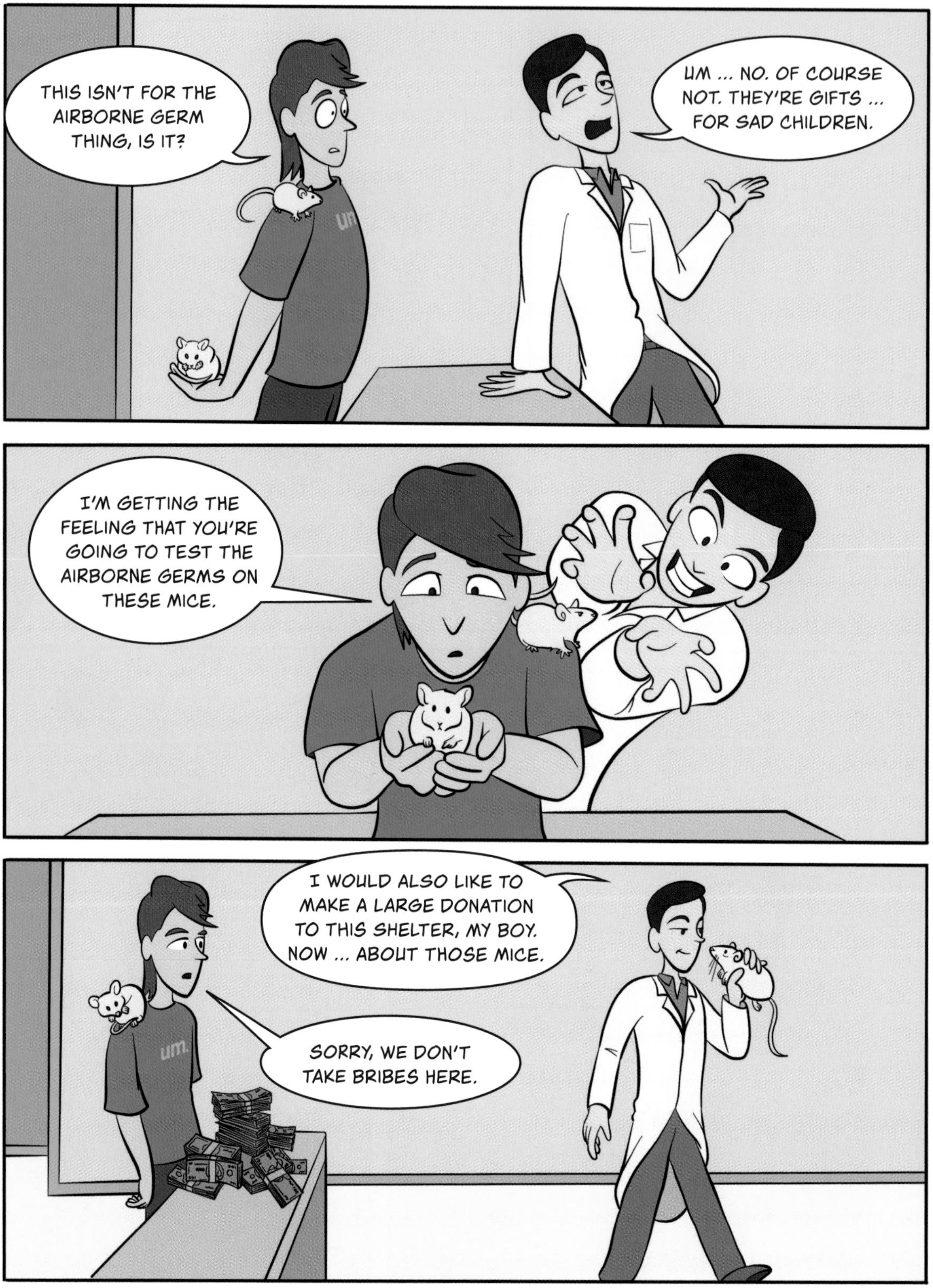
THIS ISN'T FOR THE AIRBORNE GERM THING, IS IT?
UM ... NO. OF COURSE NOT. THEY'RE GIFTS ... FOR SAD CHILDREN.
I'M GETTING THE FEELING THAT YOU'RE GOING TO TEST THE AIRBORNE GERMS ON THESE MICE.
I WOULD ALSO LIKE TO MAKE A LARGE DONATION TO THIS SHELTER, MY BOY. NOW ... ABOUT THOSE MICE.
SORRY, WE DON'T TAKE BRIBES HERE.

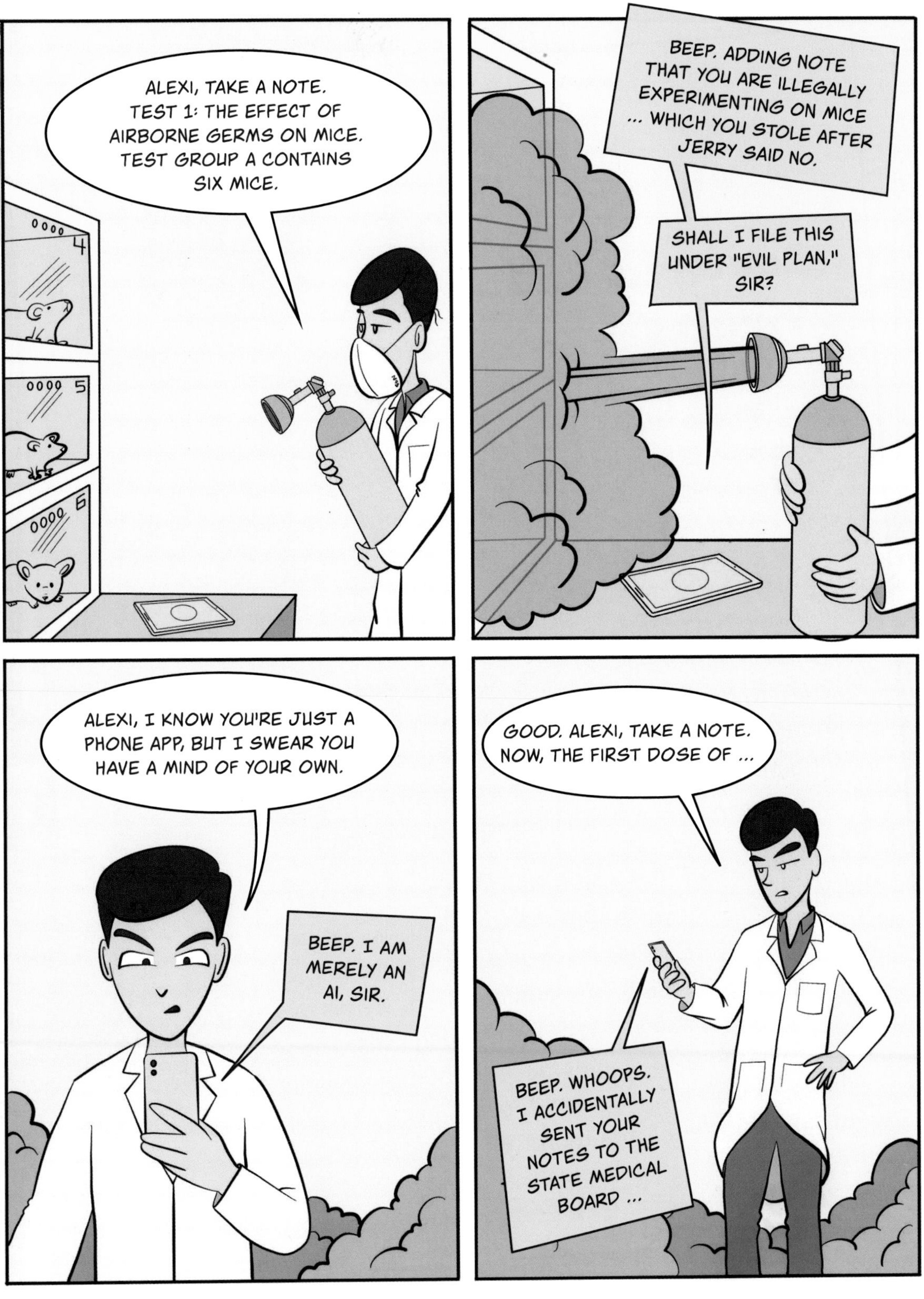
ALEXI, TAKE A NOTE. TEST 1: THE EFFECT OF AIRBORNE GERMS ON MICE. TEST GROUP A CONTAINS SIX MICE.
BEEP. ADDING NOTE THAT YOU ARE ILLEGALLY EXPERIMENTING ON MICE ... WHICH YOU STOLE AFTER JERRY SAID NO.
SHALL I FILE THIS UNDER "EVIL PLAN," SIR?
ALEXI, I KNOW YOU'RE JUST A PHONE APP, BUT I SWEAR YOU HAVE A MIND OF YOUR OWN.
BEEP. I AM MERELY AN AI, SIR.
GOOD. ALEXI, TAKE A NOTE. NOW, THE FIRST DOSE OF ...
BEEP. WHOOPS. I ACCIDENTALLY SENT YOUR NOTES TO THE STATE MEDICAL BOARD ...

Bacteria and Viruses

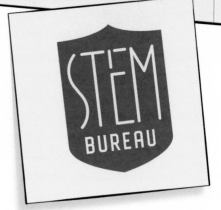

Bacteria and viruses are two types of germs that cause illnesses and infections. Bacteria can cause pneumonia or food poisoning, whereas viruses can cause the common cold and sore throats.

Bacteria are complex, single-cell creatures. They have a rigid cell wall that protects their cell membrane. Antibiotics, like penicillin, are commonly used as medicine to kill bacteria by breaking down this cell wall. However, bacteria can become **immune** to antibiotics. It is important for people to take antibiotics exactly as the doctor prescribes. Otherwise, the bacteria can become resistant to that medication.

Antibiotics do not work on viral infections since viruses behave differently and are structurally unlike bacteria. Viruses have a coating on their outside layer to protect their core genetic material. In a viral infection, a virus rapidly reproduces by attaching itself to human cells. The virus then injects its own genetic material into the human cells and tells those cells to make new viruses until it bursts and dies. Antiviral drugs are a common type of medicine used to kill viruses.

IMMUNE—ABLE TO RESIST SOMETHING, SUCH AS TREATMENT

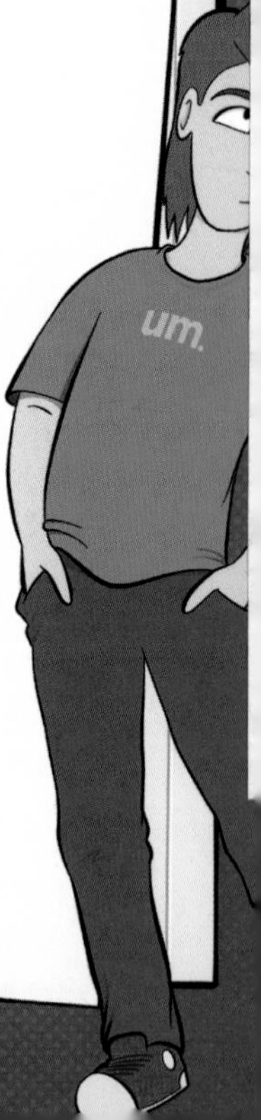
um.

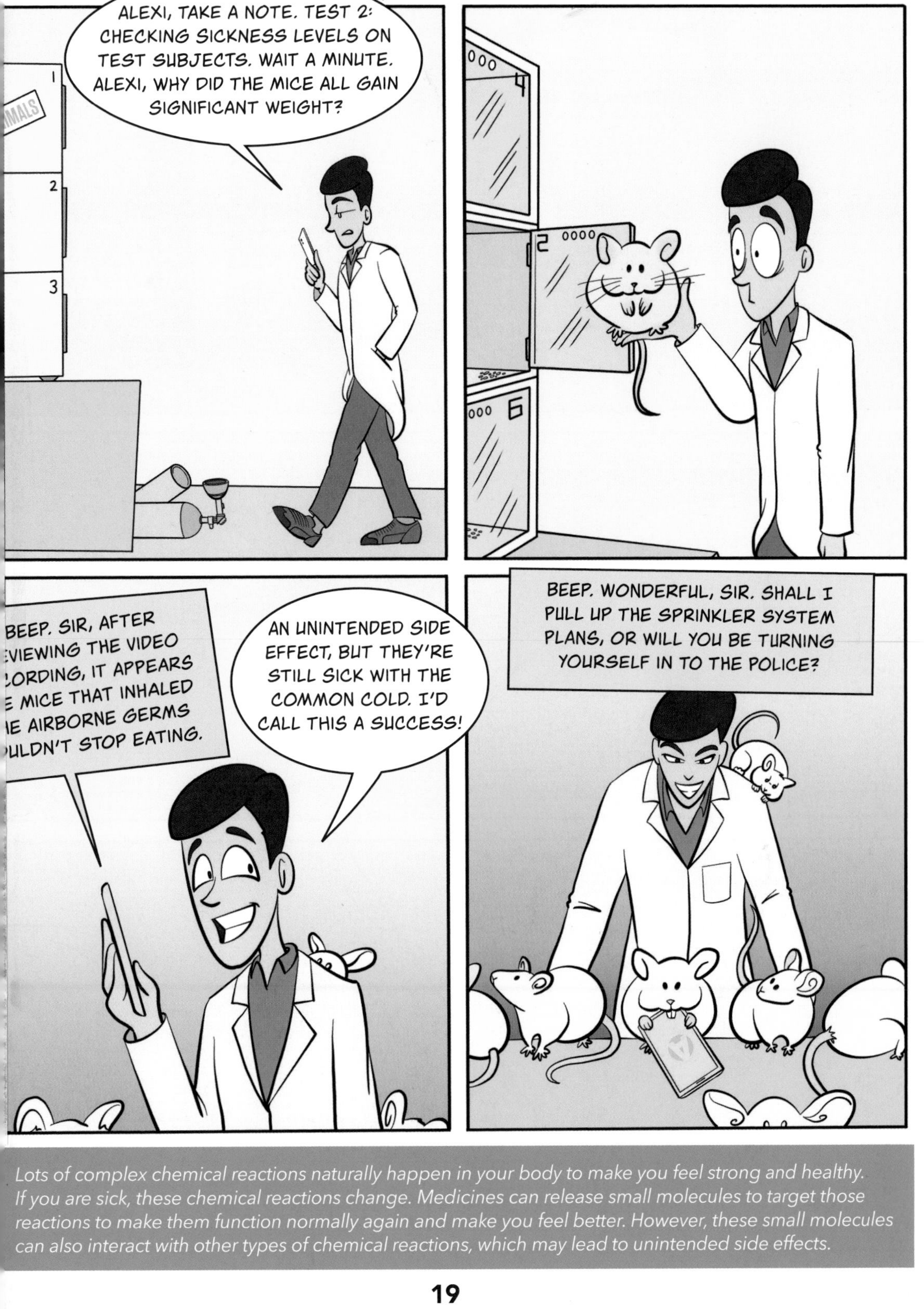
ALEXI, TAKE A NOTE. TEST 2: CHECKING SICKNESS LEVELS ON TEST SUBJECTS. WAIT A MINUTE. ALEXI, WHY DID THE MICE ALL GAIN SIGNIFICANT WEIGHT?
BEEP. SIR, AFTER EVIEWING THE VIDEO CORDING, IT APPEARS E MICE THAT INHALED IE AIRBORNE GERMS ULDN'T STOP EATING.
AN UNINTENDED SIDE EFFECT, BUT THEY'RE STILL SICK WITH THE COMMON COLD. I'D CALL THIS A SUCCESS!
BEEP. WONDERFUL, SIR. SHALL I PULL UP THE SPRINKLER SYSTEM PLANS, OR WILL YOU BE TURNING YOURSELF IN TO THE POLICE?

Lots of complex chemical reactions naturally happen in your body to make you feel strong and healthy. If you are sick, these chemical reactions change. Medicines can release small molecules to target those reactions to make them function normally again and make you feel better. However, these small molecules can also interact with other types of chemical reactions, which may lead to unintended side effects.

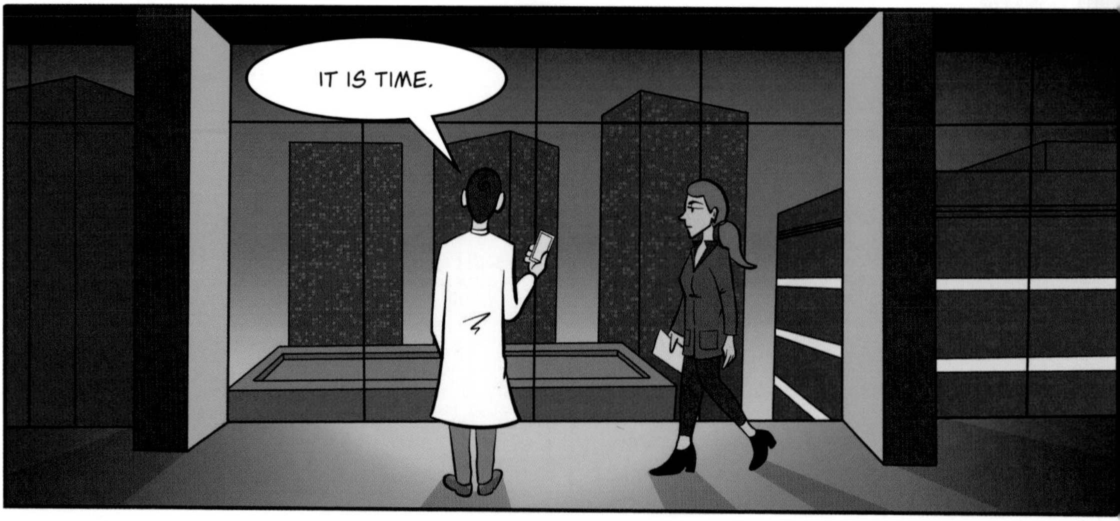
IT IS TIME.

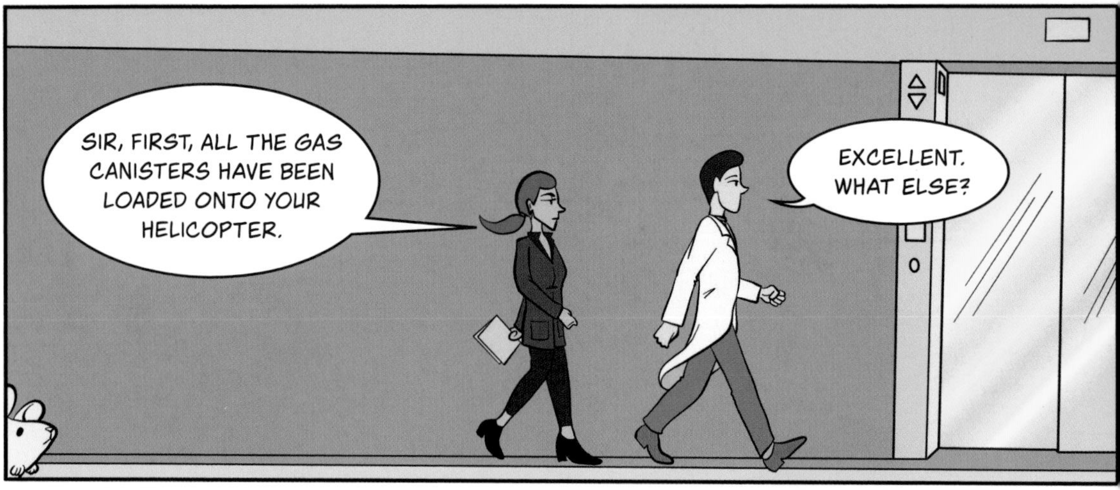
SIR, FIRST, ALL THE GAS CANISTERS HAVE BEEN LOADED ONTO YOUR HELICOPTER.
EXCELLENT. WHAT ELSE?

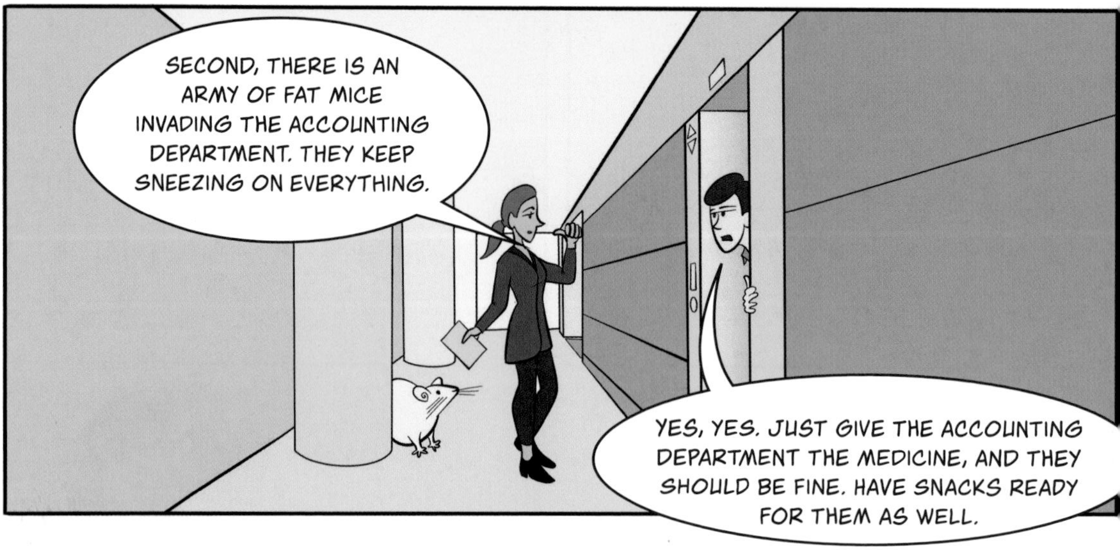
SECOND, THERE IS AN ARMY OF FAT MICE INVADING THE ACCOUNTING DEPARTMENT. THEY KEEP SNEEZING ON EVERYTHING.
YES, YES. JUST GIVE THE ACCOUNTING DEPARTMENT THE MEDICINE, AND THEY SHOULD BE FINE. HAVE SNACKS READY FOR THEM AS WELL.

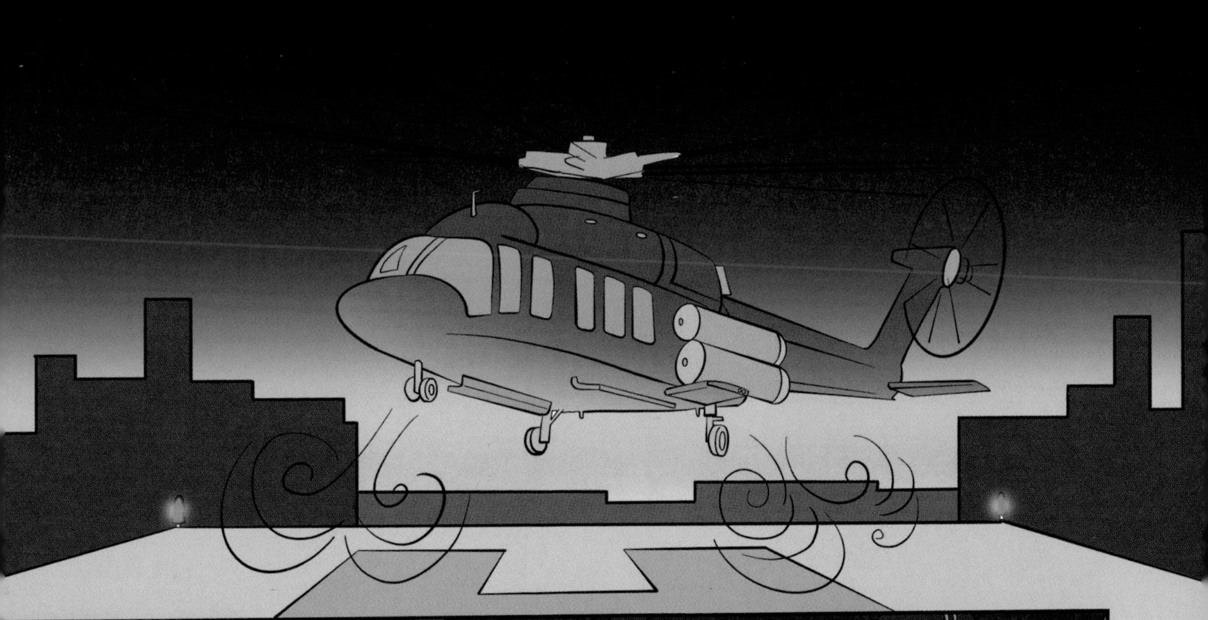

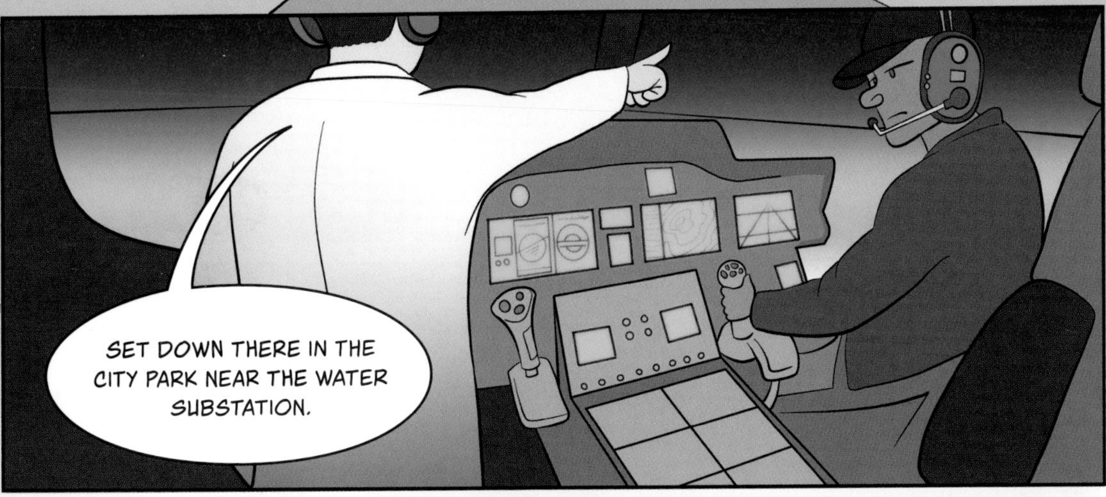
SET DOWN THERE IN THE CITY PARK NEAR THE WATER SUBSTATION.

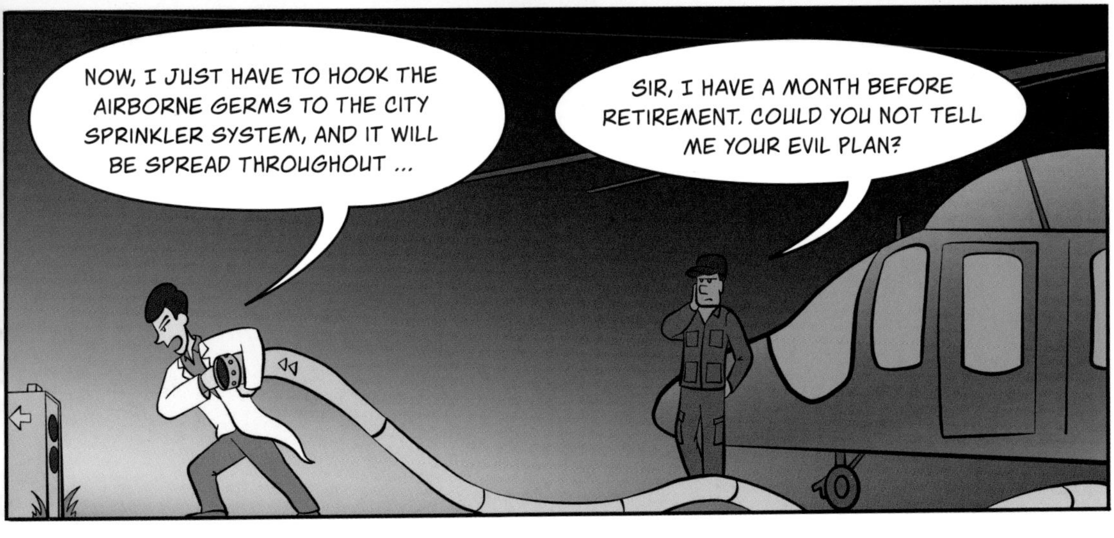
NOW, I JUST HAVE TO HOOK THE AIRBORNE GERMS TO THE CITY SPRINKLER SYSTEM, AND IT WILL BE SPREAD THROUGHOUT ...
SIR, I HAVE A MONTH BEFORE RETIREMENT. COULD YOU NOT TELL ME YOUR EVIL PLAN?

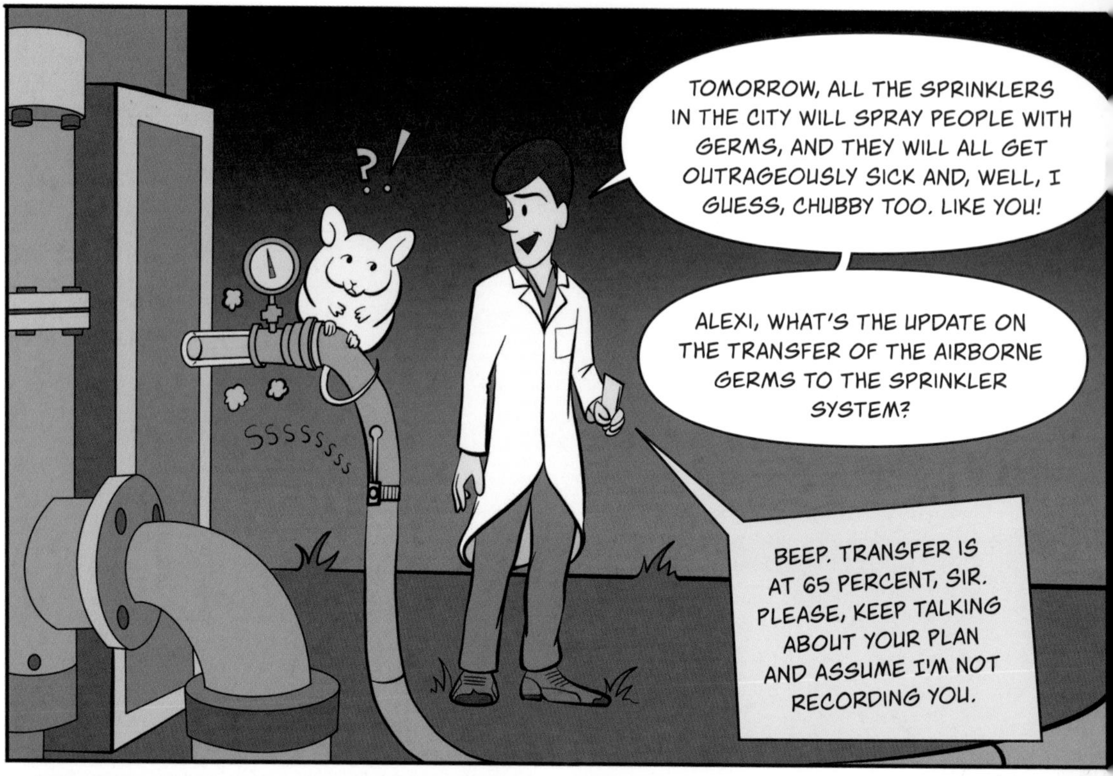
?!
TOMORROW, ALL THE SPRINKLERS IN THE CITY WILL SPRAY PEOPLE WITH GERMS, AND THEY WILL ALL GET OUTRAGEOUSLY SICK AND, WELL, I GUESS, CHUBBY TOO. LIKE YOU!
ALEXI, WHAT'S THE UPDATE ON THE TRANSFER OF THE AIRBORNE GERMS TO THE SPRINKLER SYSTEM?
SSSSSSSSS
BEEP. TRANSFER IS AT 65 PERCENT, SIR. PLEASE, KEEP TALKING ABOUT YOUR PLAN AND ASSUME I'M NOT RECORDING YOU.

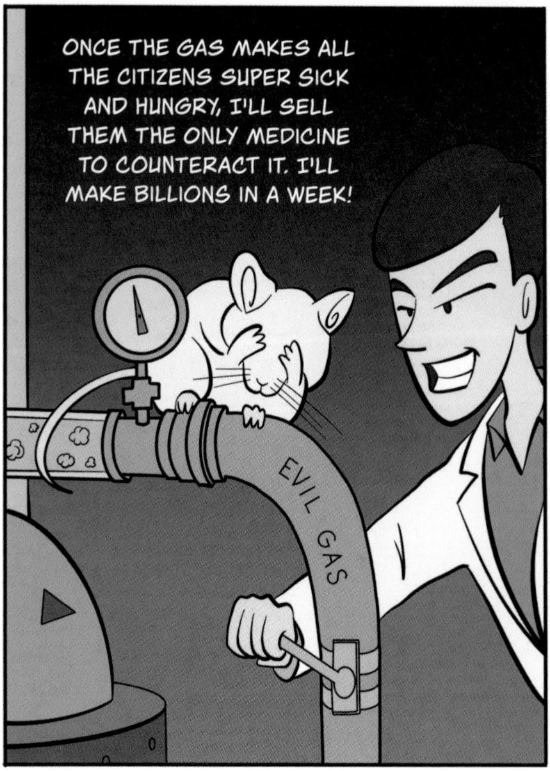
ONCE THE GAS MAKES ALL THE CITIZENS SUPER SICK AND HUNGRY, I'LL SELL THEM THE ONLY MEDICINE TO COUNTERACT IT. I'LL MAKE BILLIONS IN A WEEK!
EVIL GAS

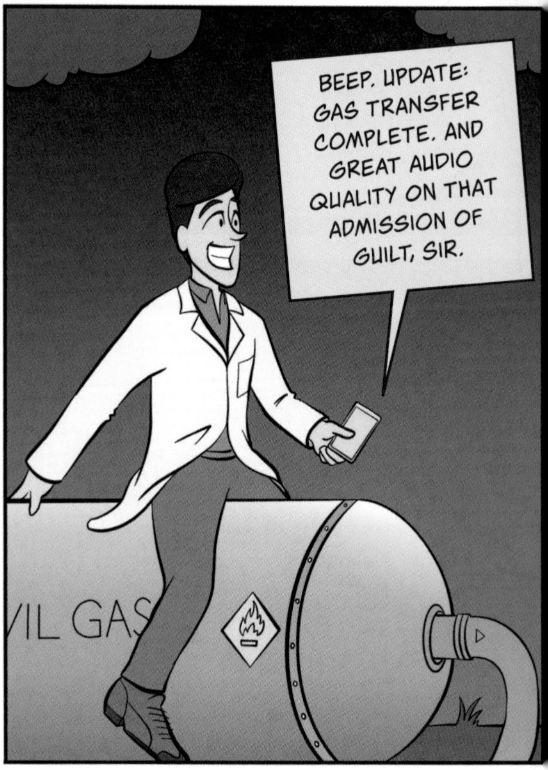
BEEP. UPDATE: GAS TRANSFER COMPLETE. AND GREAT AUDIO QUALITY ON THAT ADMISSION OF GUILT, SIR.
VIL GAS

Medicine and the Body

Pharmacology is the scientific field in which scientists and researchers study how the body absorbs and reacts to medicines. Absorption, distribution, and metabolism are three common steps the body takes after being given medicine. In absorption, medicine travels from the site of application or administration into the body's circulation. For example, when swallowing a pain reliever, the medicine travels from the mouth to the **digestive tract** and eventually to the liver, where the medicine breaks down into smaller molecules. Another example can be getting a flu shot where the medicine is delivered into the arm muscle and eventually becomes absorbed into the body. In the distribution step, the medicine travels through the bloodstream to the areas of the body where it is needed. In the last step, the medicine becomes metabolized. Here, enzymes and other chemicals in the body react with the smaller molecules and change their chemical structures by interacting with the body's chemical processes. This is when the medicine gets to work in curing the illness.

DIGESTIVE TRACT—AN ORGAN SYSTEM THAT IS RESPONSIBLE FOR INGESTING AND BREAKING DOWN FOOD

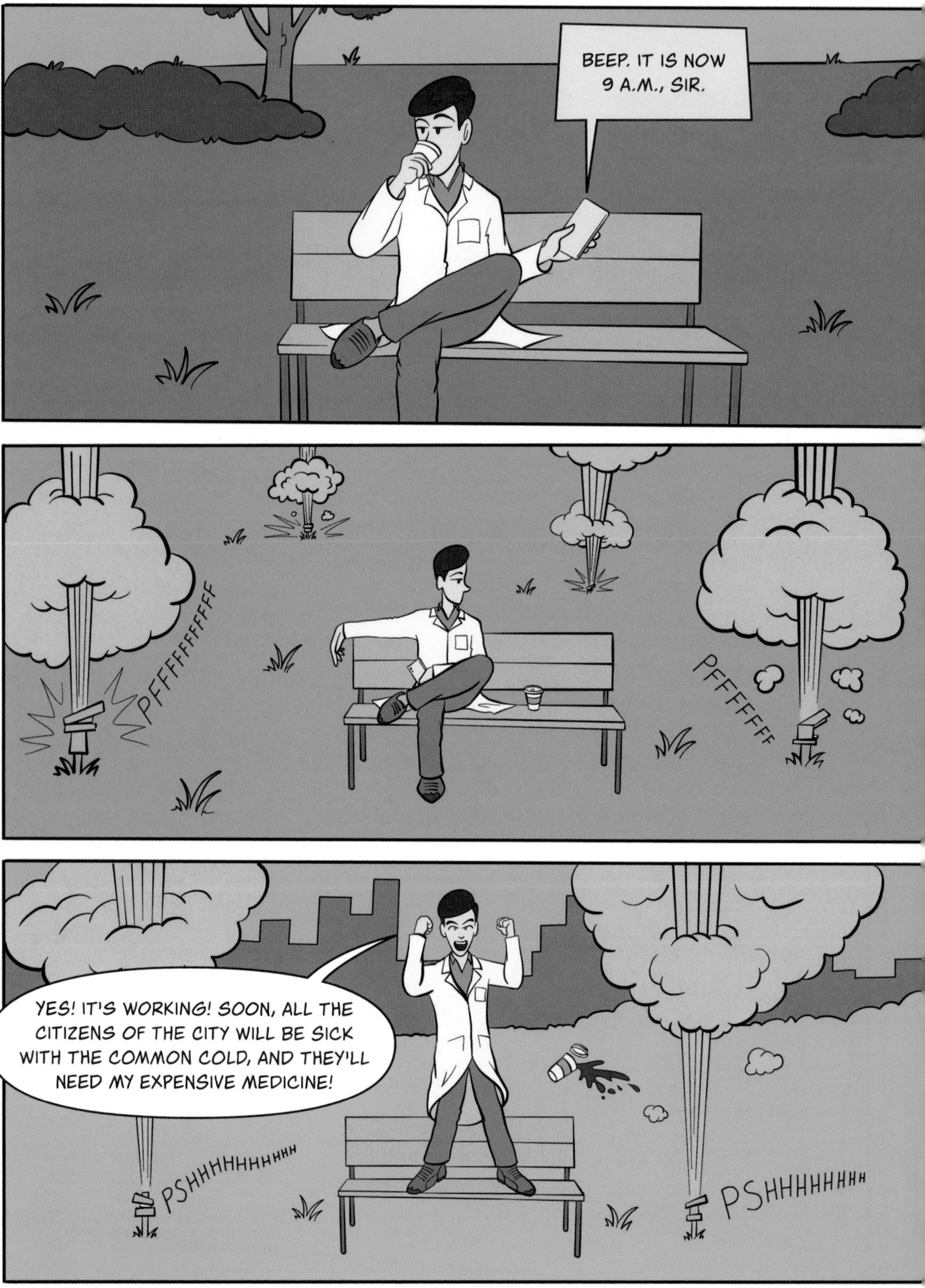
BEEP. IT IS NOW 9 A.M., SIR.
PFFFFFFFFFFFF
PFFFFFFF
YES! IT'S WORKING! SOON, ALL THE CITIZENS OF THE CITY WILL BE SICK WITH THE COMMON COLD, AND THEY'LL NEED MY EXPENSIVE MEDICINE!
PSHHHHHHHHHH
PSHHHHHHHH

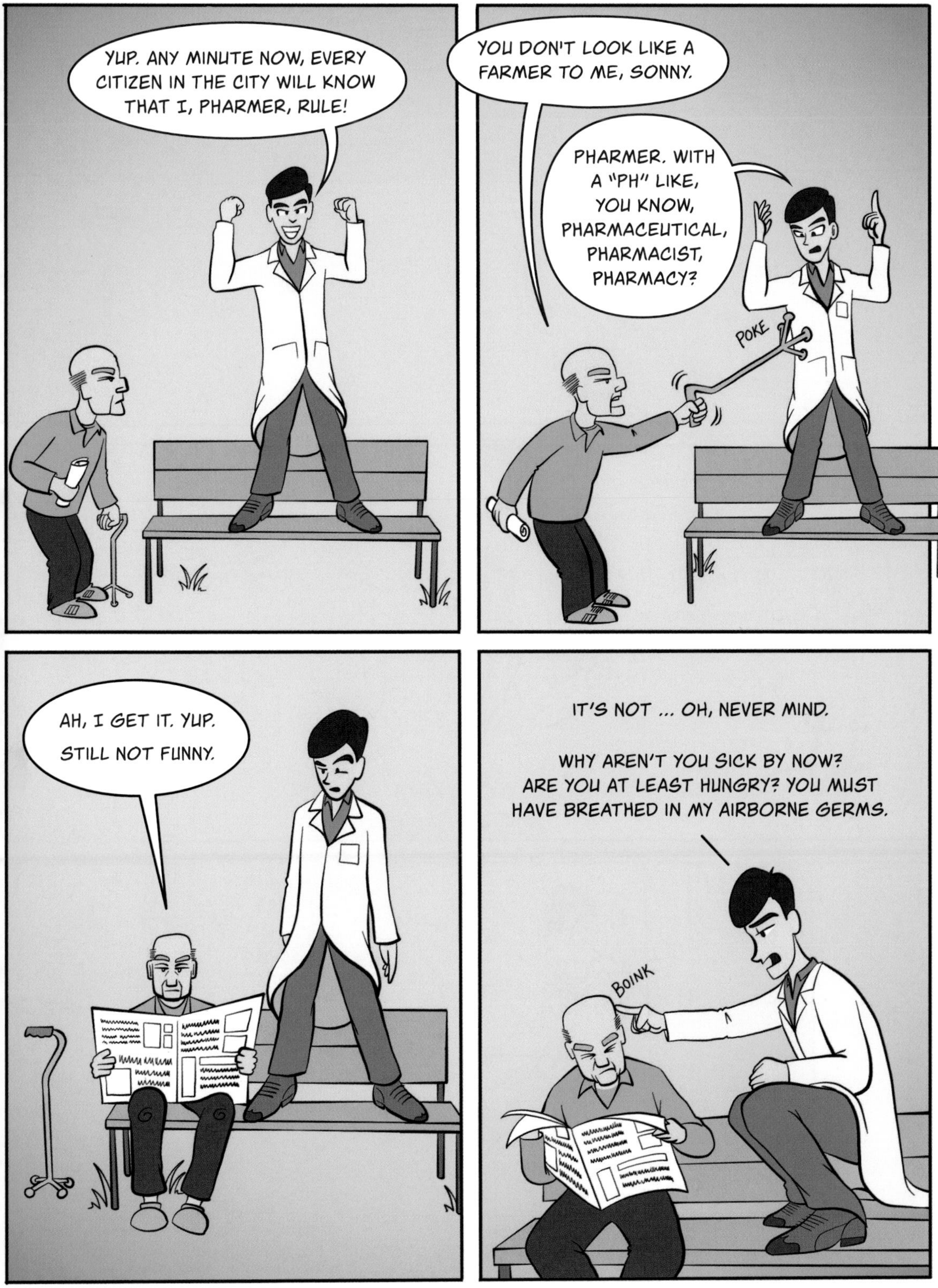
YUP. ANY MINUTE NOW, EVERY CITIZEN IN THE CITY WILL KNOW THAT I, PHARMER, RULE!
YOU DON'T LOOK LIKE A FARMER TO ME, SONNY.
PHARMER. WITH A "PH" LIKE, YOU KNOW, PHARMACEUTICAL, PHARMACIST, PHARMACY?
POKE
AH, I GET IT. YUP. STILL NOT FUNNY.
IT'S NOT ... OH, NEVER MIND.
WHY AREN'T YOU SICK BY NOW? ARE YOU AT LEAST HUNGRY? YOU MUST HAVE BREATHED IN MY AIRBORNE GERMS.
BOINK

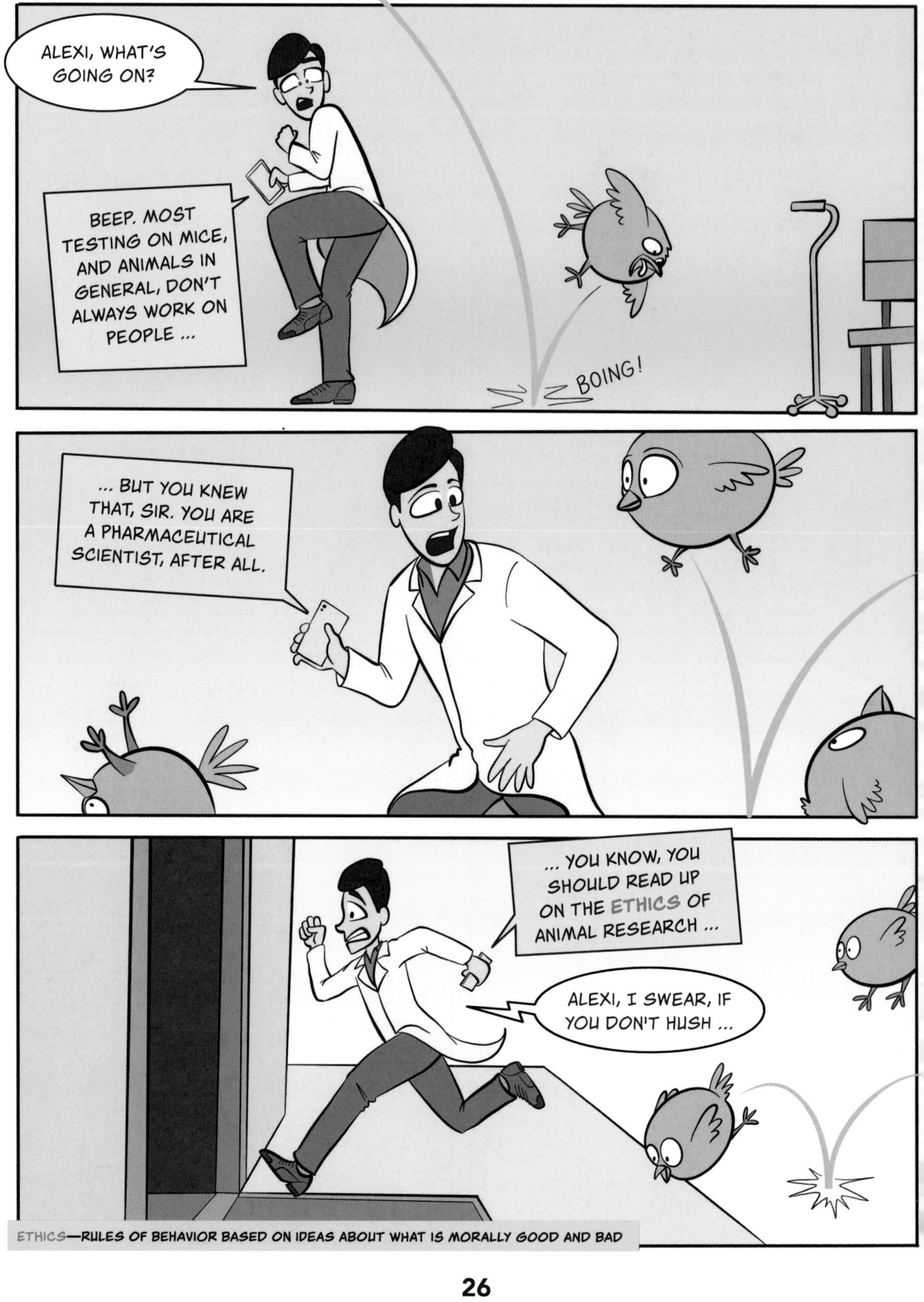
ALEXI, WHAT'S GOING ON?
BEEP. MOST TESTING ON MICE, AND ANIMALS IN GENERAL, DON'T ALWAYS WORK ON PEOPLE ...
BOING!
... BUT YOU KNEW THAT, SIR. YOU ARE A PHARMACEUTICAL SCIENTIST, AFTER ALL.
... YOU KNOW, YOU SHOULD READ UP ON THE ETHICS OF ANIMAL RESEARCH ...
ALEXI, I SWEAR, IF YOU DON'T HUSH ...

ETHICS—RULES OF BEHAVIOR BASED ON IDEAS ABOUT WHAT IS MORALLY GOOD AND BAD

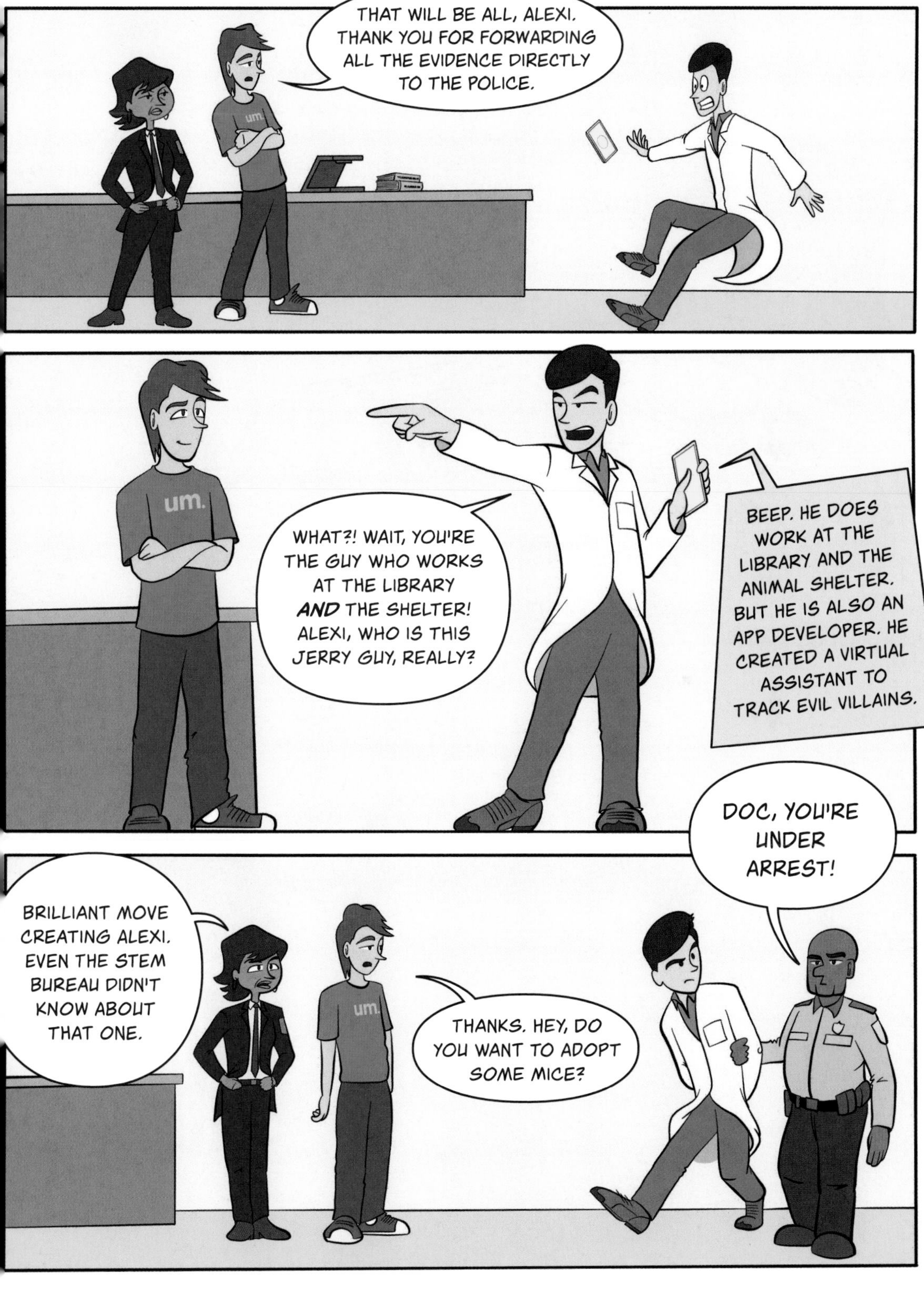
THAT WILL BE ALL, ALEXI. THANK YOU FOR FORWARDING ALL THE EVIDENCE DIRECTLY TO THE POLICE.
WHAT?! WAIT, YOU'RE THE GUY WHO WORKS AT THE LIBRARY **AND** THE SHELTER! ALEXI, WHO IS THIS JERRY GUY, REALLY?
BEEP. HE DOES WORK AT THE LIBRARY AND THE ANIMAL SHELTER. BUT HE IS ALSO AN APP DEVELOPER. HE CREATED A VIRTUAL ASSISTANT TO TRACK EVIL VILLAINS.
DOC, YOU'RE UNDER ARREST!
BRILLIANT MOVE CREATING ALEXI. EVEN THE STEM BUREAU DIDN'T KNOW ABOUT THAT ONE.
THANKS. HEY, DO YOU WANT TO ADOPT SOME MICE?

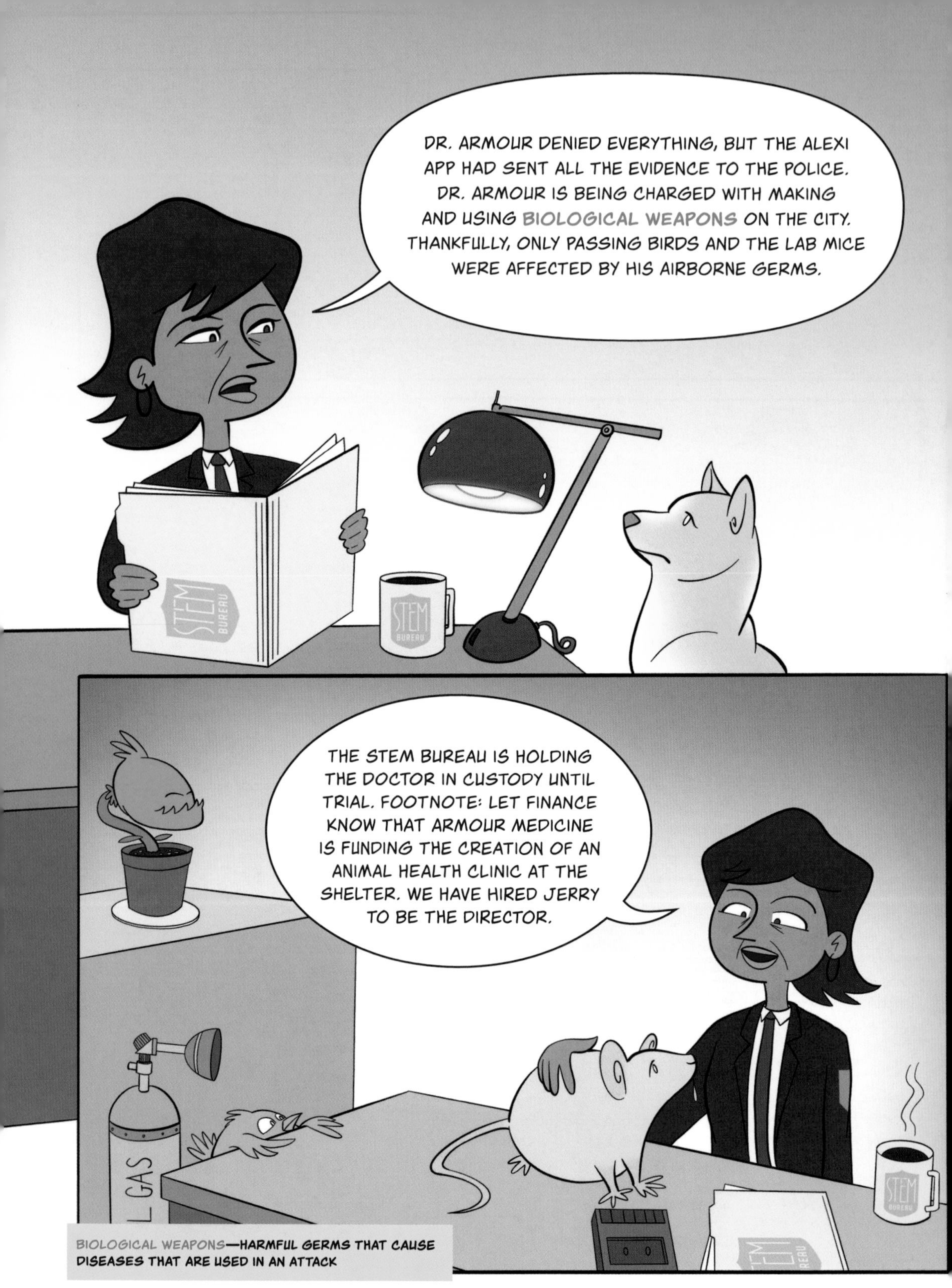
DR. ARMOUR DENIED EVERYTHING, BUT THE ALEXI APP HAD SENT ALL THE EVIDENCE TO THE POLICE. DR. ARMOUR IS BEING CHARGED WITH MAKING AND USING BIOLOGICAL WEAPONS ON THE CITY. THANKFULLY, ONLY PASSING BIRDS AND THE LAB MICE WERE AFFECTED BY HIS AIRBORNE GERMS.
THE STEM BUREAU IS HOLDING THE DOCTOR IN CUSTODY UNTIL TRIAL. FOOTNOTE: LET FINANCE KNOW THAT ARMOUR MEDICINE IS FUNDING THE CREATION OF AN ANIMAL HEALTH CLINIC AT THE SHELTER. WE HAVE HIRED JERRY TO BE THE DIRECTOR.
BIOLOGICAL WEAPONS—HARMFUL GERMS THAT CAUSE DISEASES THAT ARE USED IN AN ATTACK

EPILOGUE: VILLAIN REHABILITATION FACILITY

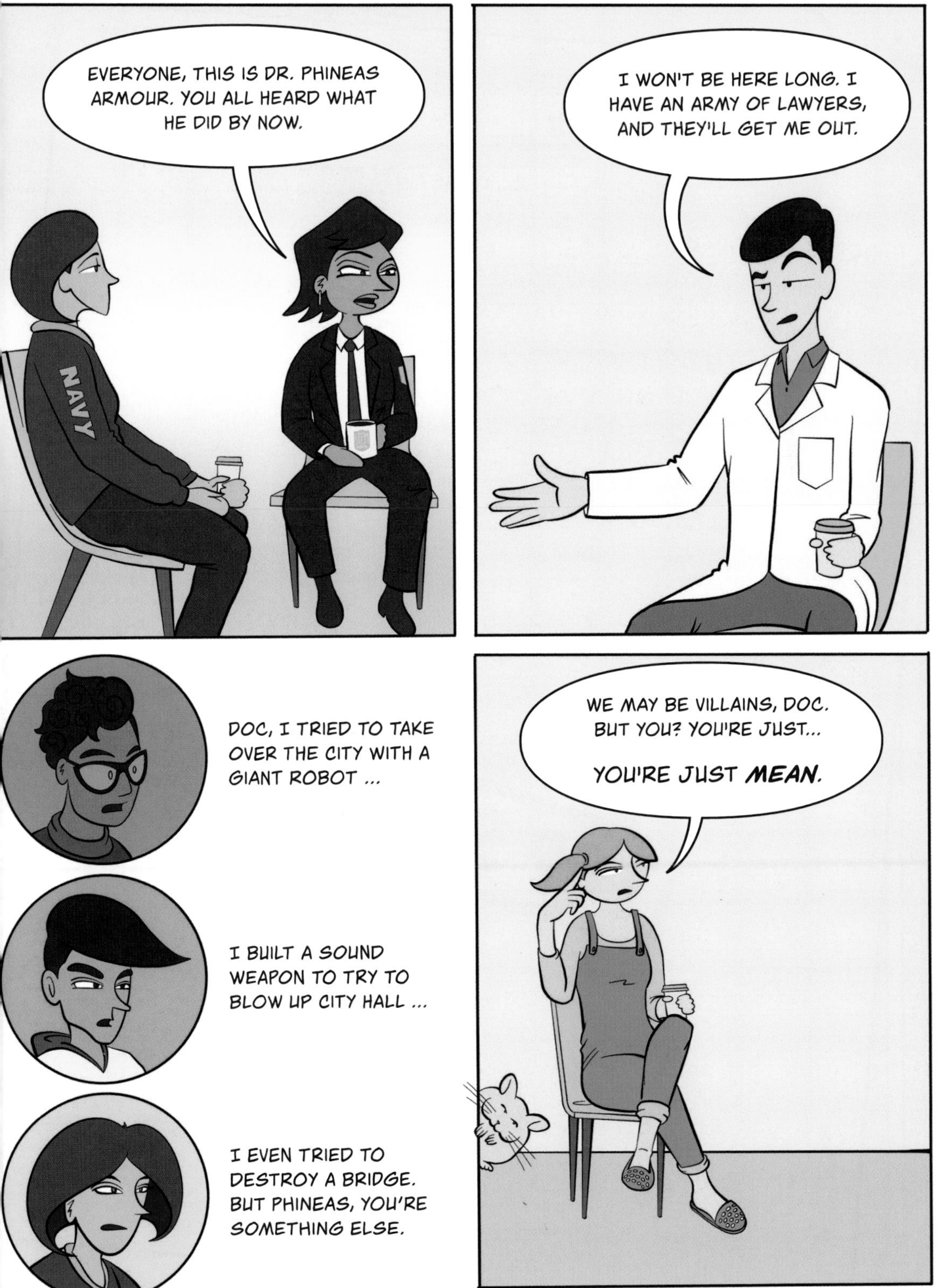
EVERYONE, THIS IS DR. PHINEAS ARMOUR. YOU ALL HEARD WHAT HE DID BY NOW.
NAVY
I WON'T BE HERE LONG. I HAVE AN ARMY OF LAWYERS, AND THEY'LL GET ME OUT.
DOC, I TRIED TO TAKE OVER THE CITY WITH A GIANT ROBOT ...
I BUILT A SOUND WEAPON TO TRY TO BLOW UP CITY HALL ...
I EVEN TRIED TO DESTROY A BRIDGE. BUT PHINEAS, YOU'RE SOMETHING ELSE.
WE MAY BE VILLAINS, DOC. BUT YOU? YOU'RE JUST...
YOU'RE JUST **MEAN.**

Medical Ethics

Practicing good ethical standards in the field of medicine and health care is very important. Every day brings more groundbreaking research and the development of new medicines that could cure diseases and cancers. However, it is important to make sure these new medicines are not harming patients or putting them in any danger. All new drugs, medications, and treatments are developed to make patients feel better. This is why large corporations and the U.S. state and federal governments have strict rules and regulations to ensure the safety of patients and their treatments. Medical professionals are responsible for following these guidelines and maintaining these standards.

Glossary

aerosolized (AIR-uh-saw-lized) made into particles small enough to move through the air

airborne germs (AIR-born JURMZ) germs that are in the air

asthma inhalers (AZ-muh in-HAY-lurz) portable medical devices used for delivering asthma medication

biological weapons (bye-uh-LAH-jih-kuhl WEP-uhnz) harmful germs that cause diseases that are used as a weapon

digestive tract (dye-JEST-iv TRAKT) an organ system that is responsible for ingesting and digesting food

ethics (ETH-iks) rules of behavior based on ideas about what is morally good and bad

immune (ih-MYOON) able to resist something, such as treatment

mitigation (mit-uh-GAY-shuhn) the act of making something less dangerous or damaging

pharmaceutical (fahr-muh-SOO-tih-kuhl) relating to medicine

reverse engineer (ri-VURS en-juh-NEER) to study the parts of something in order to know how it is made and how it works

strategic (struh-TEE-jik) useful or important in achieving a plan or strategy

ventilation (ven-tuh-LAY-shuhn) a system that moves air around a building

Index

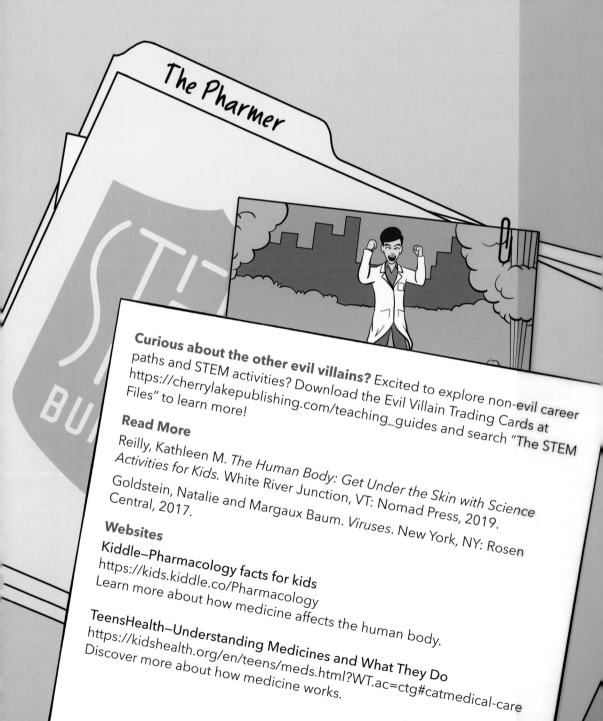

The Pharmer

Curious about the other evil villains? Excited to explore non-evil career paths and STEM activities? Download the Evil Villain Trading Cards at https://cherrylakepublishing.com/teaching_guides and search "The STEM Files" to learn more!

Read More

Reilly, Kathleen M. *The Human Body: Get Under the Skin with Science Activities for Kids.* White River Junction, VT: Nomad Press, 2019.

Goldstein, Natalie and Margaux Baum. *Viruses.* New York, NY: Rosen Central, 2017.

Websites

Kiddle—Pharmacology facts for kids
https://kids.kiddle.co/Pharmacology
Learn more about how medicine affects the human body.

TeensHealth—Understanding Medicines and What They Do
https://kidshealth.org/en/teens/meds.html?WT.ac=ctg#catmedical-care
Discover more about how medicine works.